AAT

Level 3

Diploma in Accounting

Tax Processes for Businesses FA 2021

Question Bank

For assessments from
September 2022 to December 2023

First edition 2021

ISBN 9781 5097 4372 8
eISBN 9781 5097 4280 6

British Library Cataloguing-in-Publication Data
A catalogue record for this book is available
from the British Library

Published by

BPP Learning Media Ltd
BPP House, Aldine Place
142-144 Uxbridge Road
London W12 8AA

www.bpp.com/learningmedia

Printed in the United Kingdom

Your learning materials, published by BPP
Learning Media Ltd, are printed on paper
obtained from traceable sustainable sources.

The contents of this book are intended as a
guide and not for professional advice. Although
every effort has been made to ensure that the
contents of this book are correct at the time of
going to press, BPP Learning Media makes no
warranty that the information in this book is
accurate or complete and accepts no liability
for any loss or damage suffered by any person
acting or refraining from acting as a result of
the material in this book.

We are grateful to the AAT for permission to
reproduce the sample assessment(s). The
answers to the sample assessment(s) have been
published by the AAT. All other answers have
been prepared by BPP Learning Media Ltd.

Contents

Introduction

This is BPP Learning Media's AAT Question Bank for *Tax Processes for Businesses*. It is part of a suite of ground-breaking resources produced by BPP Learning Media for AAT assessments.

This Question Bank has been written in conjunction with the BPP Course Book, and has been carefully designed to enable students to practise all of the learning outcomes and assessment criteria for the units that make up *Tax Processes for Businesses*. It is fully up to date as at September 2021 and reflects both the AAT's qualification specification and the sample assessment provided by the AAT. All questions are based on the Finance Act 2021, which is examinable to December 2022.

This Question Bank contains these key features:

- Tasks corresponding to each chapter of the Course Book. Some tasks are designed for learning purposes, others are of assessment standard.

- BPP practice assessments.

The emphasis in all tasks and assessments is on the practical application of the skills acquired.

VAT

You may find tasks throughout this Question Bank that need you to calculate or be aware of a rate of VAT. This is stated at 20% in these examples and questions.

Approaching the assessment

When you sit the assessment it is very important that you follow the on screen instructions. This means you need to carefully read the instructions, both on the introduction screens and during specific tasks.

When you access the assessment you should be presented with an introductory screen with information similar to that shown below (taken from the introductory screen from one of the AAT's AQ2022 sample assessments for *Tax Processes for Businesses*).

We have provided this **practice assessment** to help you familiarise yourself with our e-assessment environment. It is designed to demonstrate as many of the question types that you may find in a live assessment as possible. It is not designed to be used on its own to determine whether you are ready for a live assessment.

At the end of this practice assessment you will receive an immediate result.

Assessment information:

You have **90 minutes** to complete this practice assessment.

This assessment contains **8 tasks** and you should attempt to complete every task.
Each task is independent. You will not need to refer to your answers in previous tasks.
Read every task carefully to make sure you understand what is required.

Where the date is relevant, it is given in the task data.

Never use minus signs or brackets to indicate negative numbers **unless** task instructions say otherwise.

You must use a full stop to indicate a decimal point.
For example, write 100.57 NOT 100,57 or 100 57

You may use a comma to indicate a number in the thousands, but you don't have to.
For example, 10000 and 10,000 are both acceptable.

If your answer requires rounding, apply normal mathematical rounding rules **unless** the task instructions say otherwise. If your answer is a calculation of VAT and requires rounding, apply the relevant VAT rounding rules.

The actual instructions will vary depending on the subject you are studying for. It is very important you read the instructions on the introductory screen and apply them in the assessment. You don't want to lose marks when you know the correct answer just because you have not entered it in the right format.

In general, the rules set out in the AAT sample assessments for the subject you are studying for will apply in the real assessment, but you should carefully read the information on this screen again in the real assessment, just to make sure. This screen may also confirm the VAT rate used if applicable.

A full stop is needed to indicate a decimal point. We would recommend using minus signs to indicate negative numbers and leaving out the comma signs to indicate thousands, as this results in a lower number of keystrokes and less margin for error when working under time pressure. Having said that, you can use whatever is easiest for you as long as you operate within the rules set out for your particular assessment.

You have to show competence throughout the assessment and you should therefore complete all of the tasks. Don't leave questions unanswered.

In some assessments, written or complex tasks may be human marked. In this case you are given a blank space or table to enter your answer into. You are told in the assessments which tasks these are (note: there may be none if all answers are marked by the computer).

If these involve calculations, it is a good idea to decide in advance how you are going to lay out your answers to such tasks by practising answering them on a word document, and certainly you should try all such tasks in this Question Bank and in the AAT's environment using the sample assessment.

When asked to fill in tables, or gaps, never leave any blank even if you are unsure of the answer. Fill in your best estimate.

Note that for some assessments where there is a lot of scenario information or tables of data provided (eg tax tables), you may need to access these via 'pop-ups'. Instructions will be provided on how you can bring up the necessary data during the assessment.

Finally, take note of any task specific instructions once you are in the assessment. For example you may be asked to enter a date in a certain format or to enter a number to a certain number of decimal places.

Grading

To achieve the qualification and to be awarded a grade, you must pass all the mandatory unit assessments.

The AAT Level 3 Diploma in Accounting will be awarded a grade. This grade will be based on performance across the qualification. Unit assessments are not individually graded. These assessments are given a mark that is used in calculating the overall grade.

How overall grade is determined

You will be awarded an overall qualification grade (Distinction, Merit, and Pass). If you do not achieve the qualification you will not receive a qualification certificate, and the grade will be shown as unclassified.

The marks of each assessment will be converted into a percentage mark and rounded up or down to the nearest whole number. This percentage mark is then weighted according to the weighting of the unit assessment or synoptic assessment within the qualification. The resulting weighted assessment percentages are combined to arrive at a percentage mark for the whole qualification.

Grade definition	Percentage threshold
Distinction	90–100%
Merit	80–89%
Pass	70–79%
Unclassified	0–69% Or failure to pass one or more assessment/s

Re-sits

Some AAT qualifications such as the AAT Diploma in Accounting have restrictions in place for how many times you are able to re-sit assessments. Please refer to the AAT website for further details.

You should only be entered for an assessment when you are well prepared and you expect to pass the assessment.

AAT qualifications

The material in this book may support the following AAT qualifications:

AAT Level 3 Diploma in Accounting

AAT Level 3 Certificate in Bookkeeping

AAT Diploma in Accounting at SCQF Level 7

Supplements

From time to time we may need to publish supplementary materials to one of our titles. This can be for a variety of reasons. From a small change in the AAT unit guidance to new legislation coming into effect between editions.

You should check our supplements page regularly for anything that may affect your learning materials. All supplements are available free of charge on our supplements page on our website at:

www.bpp.com/learning-media/about/students

Improving material and removing errors

There is a constant need to update and enhance our study materials in line with both regulatory changes and new insights into the assessments.

From our team of authors BPP appoints a subject expert to update and improve these materials for each new edition.

Their updated draft is subsequently technically checked by another author and from time to time non-technically checked by a proofreader.

We are very keen to remove as many numerical errors and narrative typos as we can but given the volume of detailed information being changed in a short space of time we know that a few errors will sometimes get through our net.

We apologise in advance for any inconvenience that an error might cause. We continue to look for new ways to improve these study materials and would welcome your suggestions. If you have any comments about this book, the BPP author of this edition can be emailed at: learningmedia@bpp.com.

Question Bank

Chapter 1 Introduction to VAT

1.1   Black Ltd pays for goods from a supplier, and the amount includes VAT.

Is this amount of VAT to be treated as output VAT or input VAT for Black Ltd?

	✓
Output tax	
Input tax	

1.2   A VAT-registered retailer buys a product for £100 plus VAT of £20. The retailer sells the product to a member of the public for £125 plus VAT of £25.

Which ONE of the following statements is TRUE?

	✓
The retailer suffers a net cost of £5 VAT being the difference between its output and input tax on the product.	
The true cost of the product to the retailer is £120.	
The retailer does not bear any of the cost of VAT. The member of the public bears the full cost of £25 VAT.	
The retailer bears a VAT cost of £20 and the member of the public bears a VAT cost of £25.	

1.3   A trader buys a product from a manufacturer for £200 plus VAT of £40. The trader is not VAT-registered. The trader sells the product to a member of the public.

Which ONE of the following statements is TRUE?

	✓
The true cost of the product to the trader is £200.	
The trader suffers a VAT cost of £40.	
The trader accounts for output VAT of £40 on its purchase from the manufacturer.	
The member of the public suffers a VAT cost of £40.	

Chapter 2 VAT basics

2.1 Identify which ONE of the following types of supply are deemed to be taxable supplies for VAT purposes.

	✓
Standard-rated supplies only	
Standard and zero-rated supplies	
Zero-rated and exempt supplies	
All three types of supply	

2.2 Several businesses each purchased goods during a month for £13,500 plus VAT.

Identify whether each of these businesses can or cannot reclaim the input tax on the goods purchased.

TICK ONE BOX FOR EACH BUSINESS

Business	Yes, can reclaim ✓	No, cannot reclaim ✓
Bread Ltd – making only standard-rated supplies		
Soup Ltd – making only exempt supplies		
Marmalade Ltd – making only zero-rated supplies		

2.3 A VAT-registered business making only zero-rated supplies has just paid £100 plus VAT of £20 for goods.

What is the net cost of the goods to the business?

TICK ONE BOX

Cost	✓
£0	
£20	
£100	
£120	

2.4 Jam Ltd is a bus company making only zero-rated supplies.

Which ONE of the following statements is correct in relation to Jam Ltd?

	Correct
Jam Ltd cannot register for VAT.	
If Jam Ltd is VAT-registered it will make payments to HMRC.	
If Jam Ltd is VAT-registered it will have repayments from HMRC.	

2.5 Bradley's business makes taxable supplies of approximately £30,000 each year. He is considering voluntarily registering for VAT.

Identify whether the following statements are true or false in relation to voluntary registration.

TICK ONE BOX FOR EACH STATEMENT

	True	False
If Bradley's business makes zero-rated supplies, it will be in a VAT repayment position.		
If Bradley makes standard-rated supplies, it will be disadvantageous for non VAT-registered customers.		

2.6 **Identify whether the following businesses making taxable supplies need to register for VAT immediately, or monitor turnover and register later.**

TICK ONE BOX ON EACH LINE

	Register now	Monitor and register later
An existing business with a total turnover of £6,350 per month for the last 12 months.		
A new business with an expected turnover of £25,000 per month for the next 12 months.		
An existing business with a total turnover of £6,000 per month for the last 12 months. A new contract will bring in additional sales of £86,000, in 10 days' time.		

2.7 **Identify whether each of these businesses can or cannot register for VAT.**

TICK ONE BOX FOR EACH BUSINESS

	Can register	Cannot register
Blackberry Ltd – making only zero-rated supplies		
Raspberry Ltd – making standard-rated and zero-rated supplies		
Loganberry Ltd – making only exempt supplies		
Gooseberry Ltd – making standard-rated and exempt supplies		

2.8 Flan Ltd makes only zero-rated supplies.

Identify whether the following statements are true or false in relation to VAT registration.

TICK ONE BOX FOR EACH STATEMENT

	True	False
Flan Ltd cannot register as it makes only zero-rated supplies.		
Flan Ltd is automatically exempt from registering for VAT.		
Flan Ltd can register for VAT.		
Flan Ltd can apply to HMRC to be exempt from registration.		

2.9 **Identify whether the following supplies are included or excluded when considering whether the VAT registration limit has been reached.**

TICK ONE BOX ON EACH LINE

	Include	Exclude
Standard-rated supplies		
Zero-rated supplies		
Exempt supplies		

2.10 A VAT-registered trader's sales are looking like they will fall below the deregistration limit.

Complete the sentence below by selecting the appropriate number.

The trader may deregister if:

Taxable turnover in the next	▼	months is expected to fall below the deregistration limit.

Picklist:

3
12
24

2.11 **For the purpose of your assessment, which ONE of the following is the deregistration threshold?**

	✓
£85,000	
£83,000	
£150,000	
£1.35 million	

2.12 A business has exceeded the VAT registration limit in the last 12 months for the first time. However, this was because of one unusual contract which is unlikely to be repeated.

Identify whether the following statement is true or false.

	True	False
The business can apply to HMRC for exception from registration, because the level of taxable supplies was temporary.		

Chapter 3 Inputs and outputs

3.1 Below are details of two VAT invoices to be issued by a trader who makes only standard-rated supplies.

Insert the figures in the relevant columns, as appropriate.

Invoice number	Net £	VAT £	Gross £
1000325			390.60
1000326	452.92		

3.2 **Identify whether input tax can be reclaimed by a VAT-registered business in each of the following circumstances.**

TICK ONE BOX ON EACH LINE

Circumstance	Yes, can reclaim ✓	No, cannot reclaim ✓
Input tax incurred entertaining a UK client (meals provided during a meeting)		
Input tax incurred on the purchase of a van for use by a furniture repair business		
Input tax incurred providing meals on a training course for an employee		

3.3 Dish Ltd purchases all the fuel for the cars of its salesmen. The company reclaims the VAT on the fuel purchased. The salesmen also use their cars for private motoring.

Complete the sentence below by selecting the appropriate word.

On the VAT return Dish Ltd must include an amount of [▼] tax to take account of the private fuel used by salesmen.

Picklist:

input
output

3.4 A VAT-registered business has made the following purchases:

- A car for use by the sales manager for £14,200 plus VAT
- A van for use by the stores man for £10,500 plus VAT

Identify how much VAT can be reclaimed by the business.

TICK ONE BOX

	✓
Nil	
£2,840.00	
£2,100.00	
£4,940.00	

3.5 **Where a registered business makes a mixture of standard-rated, zero-rated and exempt supplies, which ONE of the following statements is correct?**

	✓
All input tax can be reclaimed.	
Only input tax relating to standard-rated supplies can be reclaimed.	
All input tax can be reclaimed provided certain *de minimis* tests are met.	
Only input tax relating to standard and zero-rated supplies can be reclaimed.	
No input tax can be reclaimed.	

3.6 Charlotte runs her own business and uses a car for both business and private miles. The fuel costs for the quarter are £200.00 exclusive of VAT. Charlotte wishes to reclaim all of the input VAT on the fuel. The relevant quarterly fuel scale charge for her car is £393.00.

Complete the sentences below by selecting the appropriate number.

Charlotte must pay output VAT of	▼

Picklist:

£393.00.
£65.50.
£78.60.

Charlotte may reclaim input VAT of	▼

Picklist:

£200.00.
£33.33.
£40.00.

3.7 Mohammed has purchased goods from an overseas supplier.

Complete the sentence below by selecting the appropriate word.

This purchase is known as an/a	▼

Picklist:

acquisition.
reverse charge.
export.
import.

3.8 James is providing services to a VAT-registered trader overseas. The services would be standard-rated if provided within the UK.

Complete the sentence below by selecting the appropriate word(s).

Because the service is business-to-business, it will be	▼

Picklist:

Exempt from VAT.
Zero-rated for VAT.
Standard-rated for VAT.
Reduced-rated for VAT.

3.9 Lucinda is exporting goods to a customer in India.

Complete the sentence below by selecting the appropriate word(s).

Goods exported to non-UK customers must be treated as	▼

Picklist:

exempt.
outside the scope of VAT.
standard-rated.
zero-rated.

3.10 Jones Ltd, a VAT-registered business, which makes standard-rated supplies, imports goods from Australia. The imported goods would be standard-rated with VAT of £3,100 if supplied in the UK.

Which ONE of the following is the net VAT position for Jones Ltd?

	Correct
VAT payable to HMRC of £3,100	
VAT reclaimed from HMRC of £3,100	
Nil net VAT effect	

3.11 A UK registered business acquires goods from France.

Which TWO of the following statements may be correct?

	✓
As this is a business-to-business supply, the French supplier does not need to charge VAT.	
The UK business will charge itself output tax for the goods on the VAT return and reclaim input tax on the same return.	
The UK business will pay output tax to HMRC at the point of entry into the UK and reclaim input tax on the next return.	
The French supplier will charge VAT on the goods and the UK business will be able to reclaim the VAT on its next return.	

Chapter 4 Accounting for VAT

4.1 Mr Green is a VAT-registered trader making standard-rated, zero-rated and exempt supplies.

Is he required to retain records of the amounts of different categories of supplies for VAT purposes?

TICK ONE BOX ON EACH LINE

	Yes	No
Standard-rated supplies		
Zero-rated supplies		
Exempt supplies		

4.2 A VAT-registered trader is required to keep adequate records to calculate the VAT due or reclaimable.

Complete the sentence below by inserting the appropriate number from the picklist.

VAT records should usually be retained for	▼	year(s).

Picklist:

2
3
6
20

4.3 Mrs Violet is VAT-registered and runs a business making both cash and credit sales and purchases.

In order to calculate the correct amount of output tax for Mrs Violet's business, which of the following accounting records will be needed?

TICK ONE BOX ON EACH LINE

	Yes	No
Sales daybook		
Purchases daybook		
Cash receipts book		
Cash payments book		

4.4 Mrs Orange is VAT-registered and runs a business making both cash and credit sales and purchases.

In order to calculate the correct amount of input tax for Mrs Orange's business, which of the following accounting records will be needed?

TICK ONE BOX ON EACH LINE

	Yes	No
Sales daybook		
Purchases daybook		
Cash receipts book		
Cash payments book		
Sales returns daybook		
Purchases returns daybook		

4.5 **Complete the sentence below by inserting the appropriate word from the picklist.**

A trader must retain a valid VAT	▼	in order to reclaim input tax.

Picklist:

invoice
purchase order

4.6 **Identify which ONE of the following details would not need to appear on a simplified or less detailed VAT invoice for a sale of less than £250.00.**

	✓
The supplier's name and address	
The date of supply	
Description of the goods/services	
The total excluding VAT	

4.7 Clipper Ltd holds the following invoices from suppliers.

(a)

VAT reg no 446 9989 57			Jupiter plc
Date: 4 January 20X0			1 London Road
Tax point: 4 January 20X0			Reading
Invoice no.			RL3 7CM
Clippers Ltd			
13 Gale Road			
Chester-le-Street			
NE1 1LB			

Sales of goods

Type	Quantity	VAT rate	Net
		%	£
Earrings @ £0.5 per unit	2,700	20	1,350.00
Earring studs @ £0.5 per unit	2,800	20	1,400.00
			2,750.00
VAT at 20%			550.00
Payable within 60 days			3,300.00
Price if paid within 10 days (net of 5% discount)			2,612.50
VAT at 20%			522.50
Payable within 10 days			3,135.00

(b)

HILLSIDE LTD

'The Glasgow Based Supplier of Quality Jewellery Items'

VAT reg no 337 4849 26

Clipper Ltd

13 Gale Road

Chester-le-Street

NE1 1LB

Invoice no. 0010

Date: 10 August 20X0

Tax point: 10 August 20X0

	£
Sale of 4,000 Jewellery boxes @ £2 per unit	8,000
VAT at 20%	1,600
Total	9,600

Terms: strictly net 30 days

(c)

GENEROUS PLC

11 Low Fell

Leeds

LS1 XY2

Clipper Ltd

13 Gale Road

Chester-le-Street

NE1 1LB

Invoice no: 2221

Date: 12 December 20X0

Tax point: 12 December 20X0

	Net	VAT	Total
	£	£	£
4,000 Earrings @ £0.5 per unit	2,000.00	400.00	2,400.00
8,000 Brooches @ £0.3125 per unit	2,500.00	500.00	3,000.00
2,500 'How to make Jewellery' books @ £2 per book	5,000.00	0.00	5,000.00
	9,500.00	900.00	10,400.00

(d)

JEWELS & CO

101 High Street, Gateshead NE2 22P

VAT reg no 499 3493 27

Date: 2 February 20X0

30 necklaces sold for £4 each totalling £120.00 including VAT at 20%.

For each of the above invoices, state whether it is a valid VAT invoice. If it is not valid identify the missing item(s).

Invoice	Valid ✓	Not valid ✓	Missing item(s)
(a)			▼
(b)			▼
(c)			▼
(d)			▼

Picklist:

Applicable rates of VAT (0% & 20%)
Invoice number
Supplier's address
Supplier's VAT registration number

4.8 **Indicate whether the following statements are true or false in relation to domestic reverse charge invoices.**

	True	False
The supplier charges VAT at the reduced rate of 5%.		
The supplier must always calculate and state the amount of VAT to be reverse-charged on the invoice.		
The customer must be registered under the Construction Industry Scheme.		
The customer must be registered for VAT.		

4.9 **Identify the circumstances in which a modified invoice is issued.**

	✓
Sale of goods by a retailer at a VAT inclusive value exceeding £250.	
Sale at a VAT inclusive value of less than £250.	
A VAT reverse charge will apply under the Construction Industry Scheme.	
Sale of goods to non-UK customers.	

4.10 Mrs Vase runs a VAT-registered wholesale business, Vase Foods. She is considering changing her current paper invoices to electronic invoices.

Which TWO of the following are required for HMRC to permit invoices to be issued electronically?

	✓
Vase Foods will need to implement procedures to ensure the authenticity and integrity of their electronic invoices.	
HMRC must receive copies of all electronic invoices issued.	
Vase foods' customers must agree to receive electronic invoices.	
Vase foods' customers must settle the invoices via bank transfer.	
The file type must enable invoices to be amended (eg Word document).	

4.11 Mr Glass has sent a credit note to a customer.

As a result of issuing this credit note, will Mr Glass have to pay more or less VAT to HMRC?

	✓
More VAT payable	
Less VAT payable	

4.12 Miss Spoon has received a credit note from a supplier.

Which ONE of the following is the effect on VAT?

	✓
Output tax will increase.	
Output tax will decrease.	
Input tax will increase.	
Input tax will decrease.	

4.13 An invoice is dispatched to a customer on 13 August and the goods are delivered the following day.

What is the tax point in this situation and is it a basic tax point or an actual tax point?

TICK ONE BOX

	✓
13 August and actual tax point	
13 August and basic tax point	
14 August and actual tax point	
14 August and basic tax point	

4.14 A customer orders goods on 13 August. The goods are delivered on 15 August and the invoice is sent to the customer on 31 August. Payment for the goods is made on 15 September.

What is the tax point of this transaction?

	✓
13 August	
15 August	
31 August	
15 September	

4.15 Below are details of the VAT exclusive (net) amounts on two VAT invoices to be issued by a trader who makes only standard-rated supplies (at 20%).

Invoice 25 – Standard-rated goods sold for £220.00 less a trade discount of 10%.

Invoice 26 – Goods sold for £200.00 with a settlement discount of 3% offered. The trader has chosen to issue an invoice showing both the discounted and undiscounted values.

Insert the figures in the relevant columns, as appropriate.

Invoice number	Shown on invoice as	
	VAT exclusive £	VAT £
25		
26 (discounted value)		
26 (undiscounted value)		

4.16 Knife Ltd has not been paid by a customer for an invoice issued some time ago. The company now wishes to claim a refund of the VAT on that invoice from HMRC. It can do so provided certain conditions are fulfilled.

Which ONE of the following is NOT a relevant condition?

	✓
Six months must have elapsed since payment was due.	
Output tax has been accounted for and paid.	
Notice must have been received from the customer's liquidators to state that it is insolvent.	
The debt must have been written-off in the accounts of Knife Ltd.	

Chapter 5 The VAT return

5.1 It is important for a VAT-registered trader to complete VAT returns regularly.

Complete the sentence below by inserting the appropriate number from the picklist.

VAT-registered traders must usually complete a VAT return every	▼	months.

Picklist:

1
3
6
12

5.2 **If input tax is greater than output tax in the VAT account, what will this result in?**

	✓
A VAT payment due to HMRC	
A VAT repayment from HMRC	

5.3 Cordelia's business has sales of approximately £200,000. She uses Making Tax Digital and pays by BACS.

(a) **By what date should the VAT return to 31 May 20X0 be submitted?**

	✓
30 June 20X0	
7 July 20X0	
10 July 20X0	

(b) **By what date should any tax due for the return to 31 May 20X0 be paid?**

	✓
30 June 20X0	
7 July 20X0	
10 July 20X0	

5.4 Charlotte's business has sales of approximately £200,000. She uses Making Tax Digital and pays her VAT by direct debit.

(a) **By what date should the VAT return to 31 May 20X0 be submitted?**

	✓
30 June 20X0	
7 July 20X0	
10 July 20X0	

(b) **By what date would any tax due for the return to 31 May 20X0 be paid?**

	✓
30 June 20X0	
7 July 20X0	
10 July 20X0	

5.5 Happy Ltd is able to reclaim bad debt relief on an unpaid invoice.

(a) **Which ONE of the following statements is correct?**

	✓
Input tax reclaimable will be increased and the bad debt VAT will be included in box 4 on the VAT return.	
Output tax payable will be decreased and the bad debt will VAT be included as a deduction in box 1 on the VAT return.	

Unhappy Ltd reclaims all the input tax on petrol provided to an employee for both business and private use, and will account for the private element of this by using the fuel scale charge.

(b) **Which ONE of the following statements is correct?**

	✓
Output tax payable will be increased and the fuel scale charge will be included in box 1 on the VAT return.	
Input tax reclaimable will be decreased and the fuel scale charge will be included as a deduction in box 4 on the VAT return.	

5.6 The following accounts have been extracted from the business ledgers of a VAT registered business. You have been asked to reconcile the accounting records to the business's Making Tax Digital VAT return software.

Sales account

Date 20XX	Reference	Debit £	Date 20XX	Reference	Credit £
			1.10–31.12	Sales daybook – UK sales	9,000.00
			1.10–31.12	Sales daybook – exports	3,550.00
31.12	Balance c/d	17,600.00	1.10–31.12	Cash book – UK sales	5,050.00
	Total	17,600.00		Total	17,600.00

Purchases and purchases returns account

Date 20XX	Reference	Debit £	Date 20XX	Reference	Credit £
1.10–31.12	Purchases daybook – UK purchases	2,250.00	1.10–31.12	Purchases returns daybook – UK purchases	975.00
1.10–31.12	Purchases daybook – imports	4,700.00	31.12	Balance c/d	5,975.00
	Total	6,950.00		Total	6,950.00

VAT account

Date 20XX	Reference	Debit £	Date 20XX	Reference	Credit £
1.10–31.12	Purchases daybook	450.00	1.10–31.12	Sales daybook	1,800.00
			1.10–31.12	Cash book – UK sales	1,010.00
			1.10–31.12	Purchases returns daybook – UK purchases	195.00

The business's imports are goods that would normally be standard-rated, and the business has chosen to use postponed accounting for imports.

(a) Complete the following:

The figure for VAT due on imports under postponed accounting is:	£	

(b) Complete the following:

The figure for box 1 of the VAT return is:	£	

(c) Complete the following:

The figure for box 4 of the VAT return is:	£	

(d)   The VAT return software shows output VAT in Box 1 of £2,810.00. What is the most likely cause of this discrepancy?

	✓
The flat rate scheme has been applied.	
The VAT software has been set up to apply the cash accounting scheme.	
VAT on imports has yet to be accounted for on the VAT return software.	
The VAT software has accounted for VAT on the business's UK sales at the reduced rate.	

5.7   The following accounts have been extracted from a business's ledgers for quarter ended 30 June 20X1.

Sales daybook summary

	Zero-rated sales	Standard-rated sales	VAT	Total
UK sales	17,000.00	29,500.00	5,900.00	52,400.00

Sales returns daybook summary

	Standard-rated sales	VAT	Total
UK sales	2,500.00	500.00	3,000.00

Purchases daybook summary

	Standard-rated purchases	VAT on UK purchases	Imports	Total
Purchases/expenses	13,225.00	2,645.00	2,140.00	18,010.00

Purchases returns daybook summary

	Standard-rated purchases	VAT	Total
UK purchases	1,700.00	340.00	2,040.00

In June 20X1 a bad debt was written off as irrecoverable in the business's accounting records. The debt was for £720 (VAT-inclusive) on an invoice dated 27 November 20X0. Payment terms for the business are strictly 30 days from date of invoice.

The imports are goods that would normally be standard-rated, and are to be accounted for via postponed accounting.

The Making Tax Digital software has produced the following draft VAT return figures:

VAT return for quarter ended 30.6.20X1		£
VAT due in this period on **sales** and other outputs	Box 1	5,400.00
VAT due in the period on acquisitions of goods made in Northern Ireland from EU Member States	Box 2	0.00
Total VAT due **(the sum of boxes 1 and 2)**	Box 3	5,400.00
VAT reclaimed in the period on **purchases** and other inputs, including imports	Box 4	2,305.00
Net VAT to be paid to HM Revenue & Customs or reclaimed by you **(difference between boxes 3 and 4)**	Box 5	3,095.00
Total value of **sales** and all other outputs excluding any VAT	Box 6	44,000
Total value of purchases and all other inputs excluding any VAT	Box 7	13,665

Which of the following figures have been omitted from the VAT return software?

	✓
Bad debt relief	
Purchases returns	
VAT on imports	
Sales returns	

Chapter 6 VAT schemes for small businesses

6.1 Declan has heard that there is a special scheme available to some businesses that requires only one VAT return to be prepared each year.

Complete the sentences below by selecting/inserting the appropriate words/number.

Businesses submit only one return each year if they operate the	▼	scheme.

Picklist:

annual accounting
cash accounting
flat rate

To join, taxable supplies in the next 12 months must be below £	▼

Picklist:

150,000
230,000
1,350,000
1,600,000

6.2 **Complete the sentence below by selecting the appropriate words.**

A business gets automatic bad debt relief if it operates the	▼	scheme.

Picklist:

annual accounting
cash accounting ∧
flat rate

6.3 Harry operates the flat rate scheme for his business.

Complete the sentence below by selecting the appropriate word.

Harry's VAT payable is calculated as a percentage of the VAT	▼	turnover.

Picklist:

exclusive ↑
inclusive

6.4 Debbie has a business with a year ended 30 April 20X0. Debbie operates the annual accounting scheme and has not chosen to use quarterly VAT payments.

Which ONE of the following statements is correct?

	✓
She pays some of her VAT by monthly instalments with the balance due by 31 May 20X0.	
She pays some of her VAT by monthly instalments with the balance due by 30 June 20X0.	
She pays all of her VAT in a single payment by 31 May 20X0.	
She pays all of her VAT in a single payment by 30 June 20X0.	

6.5 Donald operates the cash accounting scheme.

Identify whether the following statements are true or false in relation to the cash accounting scheme.

TICK ONE BOX ON EACH LINE

	True	False
VAT is accounted for on the basis of cash paid and received rather than on invoices.		
The scheme is advantageous for businesses making only zero-rated supplies.		
Businesses must leave the scheme if taxable supplies in the previous 12 months exceed £1,350,000.		

6.6 Jack operates the flat rate scheme.

Identify whether the following statements are true or false in relation to the flat rate scheme.

TICK ONE BOX ON EACH LINE

	True	False
Businesses issue normal VAT invoices to customers.		
VAT is paid in instalments.		
The flat rate percentage applied always depends on the type of business.		
Less VAT may be payable by Jack as a result of operating the scheme.		

6.7 Would a business that gives its customers long periods of credit, but pays its suppliers promptly benefit from operating under the cash accounting scheme?

	✓
Yes, because output VAT would be paid later and input VAT would be reclaimed at the same time or earlier.	
No, because input VAT would be reclaimed later and output VAT would be paid at the same time or earlier.	

6.8 Alex is a VAT registered trader who operates the flat rate scheme. He is defined as a 'limited cost trader'.

His sales for the quarter ended 31 March 2022 are as follows:

Standard-rated	£18,000 (net)
Zero-rated	£12,000

He also acquired the following fixed assets in the period:

Computer equipment costing	£1,200 (net)
Shop fittings costing	£3,000 (net)

What is Alex's VAT payable for the quarter?

	✓
£5,544.00	
£4,950.00	
£4,944.00	
£4,704.00	

Chapter 7 Payroll systems

7.1   Mr Pick has run a business as a sole trader for two years. His business has grown and he now plans to take on three employees, each of whom will be paid monthly and will earn in excess of the National Insurance lower earnings limit. The first pay date is likely to be 28 August 2022.

Mr Pick must register with HMRC for payroll taxes between [＿＿＿＿＿] **and** [＿＿＿＿＿]

7.2   **Identify whether the following statements concerning payroll records are true or false:**

	True	False
HMRC require employers to keep records of employees' leave and sickness absence		
Payroll records for the tax year 2021/22 must be kept until 5 April 2028		
Employee pay records are personal data and as such their storage is governed by GDPR		
HMRC may make an unannounced visit to an employer's premises to inspect payroll records		

7.3   Neck Ltd employs Mrs String. Her annual salary is £24,000, paid monthly on the 28th of each month. Neck Ltd pays its taxes electronically via bank transfer.

Payroll software is used by Neck Ltd, and the following information has been generated in respect of Mrs String for the month of June 2021:

	£
Income tax	195
Employee's NIC	140
Employer's NIC	175
Employee's pension contributions	100
Employer's pension contributions	150
Season ticket loan repayment	125

Complete the following sentences:

(a)   Mrs String's gross pay for June 2021 is £ [＿＿＿＿＿]

(b)   Mrs String's net pay for June 2021 is £ [＿＿＿＿＿]

(c)   Neck Ltd must pay £ [＿＿＿＿＿] to HMRC in respect of Mrs String's pay for the month of June 2021, on or before [＿＿＿＿＿]

7.4 Indicate which TWO of the following statements are correct in relation to the use and functions of payroll software:

	True	False
Payroll software is used to provide information to HMRC under Real Time Information (RTI).		
Payroll software can calculate statutory maternity pay.		
All payroll software that is tested and approved by HRMC will be suitable for any business.		
Once installed, payroll software will never need to be updated.		

7.5 Use the picklist to identify the function of the following payroll forms and returns:

Form	Function
Full Payment Submission (FPS)	▼
P11D	▼
P45	▼
P60	▼

Picklist:

Details of employee leaving
End of year summary of pay and deductions
End of year summary of taxable benefits
Calculation of employer Class 1A NIC
Return showing pay and deductions for each employee on a specific payment date

7.6 Fret plc paid its annual Class 1A National Insurance liability for 2021/22 electronically to HMRC on 14 July 2022. On the same day it provided all its employees with their P11D forms.

Complete the following sentences:

(a) The payment was made [late/on time]

(b) The forms were provided [late/on time]

7.7 A Full Payment Submission (FPS) form must be filed with HMRC every [ ] .

An Employer Payment Summary (EPS) must be filed every [ ] where no employees are paid.

Picklist:

day
month
year
time employees are paid

BPP LEARNING MEDIA

7.8 Jack has received his P60 form for the tax year 2021/22, showing the following figures:

	Pay £	Tax deducted £
In previous employments	0	0
In this employment	35,000.00	4,486.00
Total	35,000.00	4,486.00

National Insurance contributions in this employment

NIC table letter	Earnings at the Lower Earnings Limit (LEL) (where earnings are equal to or exceed the LEL) £	Earnings above the LEL, up to and including the Primary Threshold (PT) £	Earnings above the PT, up to and including the Upper Earnings Limit (UEL) £	Employee's contributions due on all earnings above the PT £ p
A	6,240	3,328	25,432	3,051.84

Student Loan deductions in this employment: £156.00

Required:

Complete the table below to calculate Jack's take-home (net) pay from the information provided on his P60.

Provide your answer to the nearest penny.

	£
Gross pay per P60 in 2021/22	
▼	
▼	
▼	
Take-home pay	

Picklist options:

PAYE
Employee's national insurance contributions
Employer's National Insurance contributions
Student loan deductions
Earnings at the lower earnings limit

Chapter 8 VAT and PAYE Administration

8.1 You have discovered an error on the VAT return of a client.

You adjust for this error on the next VAT return if it is which ONE of the following?

	✓
More than the error correction reporting threshold, but not deliberate	
Less than the error correction reporting threshold and not deliberate	
More than the error correction reporting threshold and was deliberate	
Less than the error correction reporting threshold, but was deliberate	

8.2 Amy's business has made a large error that exceeded the error correction reporting threshold, but was not careless or deliberate.

Identify whether the following statements are true or false in relation to this large error.

	True	False
Amy can adjust this on her next return.		
Amy cannot adjust this error on her next return and will be liable for a penalty.		

8.3 A business has made a small understatement of input tax in a previous quarter that is below the error correction threshold.

Should this adjustment be shown on the latest VAT return, and if so where on the return?

	✓
No – not shown on the return	
Yes – shown in box 1	
Yes – shown in box 4	

8.4 Abdul has just submitted his VAT return late. He has previously sent in all VAT returns on time.

For the purpose of your assessment, which ONE of the following statements is correct?

	✓
No action will be taken by HMRC.	
HMRC will issue a surcharge liability notice.	
HMRC will issue a surcharge liability notice and charge a penalty.	
HMRC charge a penalty only.	

8.5 **Complete the sentence below by selecting the appropriate number.**

A business has a requirement to retain VAT records for	▼	years.

Picklist:

three
four
six
ten

8.6 Rachel employs 15 people in her sole trader business. She pays her employees weekly. Her most recent Full Payment Submission (FPS) for the week to 14 February 20X1 was sent to HMRC on 21 February 20X1, a week after her employees had been paid. She had already filed two late FPS in the tax year, however she had always paid the relevant payroll taxes on time. Rachel deliberately omitted from her payroll software details of a cash bonus paid to each employee in the week.

Rachel paid the payroll tax in respect of the tax month 6 February 20X1 to 5 March 20X1 electronically on 15 March 20X1.

Which of the following penalties may apply to Rachel in respect of the above events?

	✓
A late filing penalty of £100	
A late filing penalty of £200.	
A late payment penalty of 1%.	
A penalty of up to 70% of underpaid tax.	

8.7 Tax avoidance is illegal and consists of seeking to pay too little tax by deliberately misleading HMRC.

Decide whether this statement is true or false.

	✓
True	
False	

8.8 Your client is Howard, who is currently VAT-registered. Howard's business is affected by a change in the VAT registration limits. Until now your client has had to be VAT-registered. However, the business has slowed down and the VAT registration/deregistration limits have increased. As a result your client could choose to deregister. The majority of the client's customers are members of the general public and not VAT-registered.

Assume today's date is 1 June 20X0.

Draft an email to your client advising him of the options available to him.

To: [▼] (1)

From: [▼] (2)

Date: [▼] (3)

Subject: [▼] (4)

Please be advised that the current level of your business turnover is such that you are able to VAT [▼] (5) As you will no longer need to charge [▼] (6) VAT to your customers, there are two options open to you.

1. Your selling prices can decrease to the VAT-exclusive amount

   As a result your profits will [▼] (7) At the same time your

   customer will have [▼] (8) cost.

2. Your selling prices can stay at the same VAT-inclusive amount

   As a result your profits will [▼] (9) At the same time your

   customer will have [▼] (10) cost.

If you wish to discuss this further please feel free to make an appointment.

Kind regards

Picklist:

(1) Howard / AN Accountant
(2) Howard / AN Accountant
(3) 1 June 20X0 / 31 March 20X0
(4) VAT rates / VAT deregistration
(5) register. / deregister.
(6) input / output
(7) increase. / decrease. / stay the same.
(8) the same / a higher / a lower
(9) increase. / decrease. / stay the same.
(10) the same / a higher / a lower

8.9　It is 1 October 20X0 and you work for a firm of accountants, ABC & Co. Your client Mr Jones is considering joining the annual accounting scheme. Mr Jones's business operates from Unit 1 Alias Industrial Estate, Chelmsford, Essex, CM2 3FG.

You have been asked to complete the letter to Mr Jones explaining how the annual accounting scheme operates.

ABC & Co
2 Smith Street
London
W1 2DE

1 October 20X0

Mr Jones
Unit 1 Alias Industrial Estate
Chelmsford
Essex
CM2 3FG

Dear [＿＿＿＿＿▼] (1)

[＿＿＿＿＿＿＿▼] (2) **(subject)**

Further to our telephone conversation of today, I have set out below the details relating to the annual accounting scheme.

Your business can join the annual accounting scheme if the value of its taxable supplies [＿＿＿＿▼] (3) VAT, in the forthcoming [＿＿＿＿＿▼] (4) months does not exceed £[＿＿＿▼] (5)

Under this scheme the business usually makes [＿＿＿＿▼] (6) equal monthly instalments. Each of these instalments is [＿＿＿＿▼] (7) of the prior year VAT liability. The first payment is due at the [＿＿＿▼] (8) of the [＿＿＿▼] (9) month of the accounting period.

The balancing payment and the VAT return will be sent to HMRC within [＿＿＿＿＿▼] (10) of the end of the accounting period.

I hope that this has clarified the position. If you wish to discuss this further please do not hesitate to contact me.

Yours sincerely

Picklist:

(1)　Mr Jones / ABC & Co
(2)　Annual accounting scheme / Cash accounting scheme
(3)　including / excluding
(4)　3 / 12
(5)　150,000 / 1,350,000 / 1,600,000
(6)　four / nine / ten
(7)　¼ / 1/10
(8)　beginning / end
(9)　first / third / fourth
(10)　30 days / a month and seven days / two months

Answer Bank

Chapter 1 Introduction to VAT

1.1   The correct answer is:

Output tax	
Input tax	✓

1.2   The correct answer is:

	✓
The retailer suffers a net cost of £5 VAT being the difference between its output and input tax on the product.	
The true cost of the product to the retailer is £120.	
The retailer does not bear any of the cost of VAT. The member of the public bears the full cost of £25 VAT.	✓
The retailer bears a VAT cost of £20 and the member of the public bears a VAT cost of £25.	

Provided the retailer makes only taxable supplies, it can recover its input VAT of £20 on its purchase, and so suffers no VAT cost. The cost of the product to the retailer is therefore £100.

The retailer will collect £25 output VAT from the customer and pay it to HMRC but it suffers no VAT cost itself. The member of the public, the final consumer, suffers the full VAT of £25.

1.3   The correct answer is:

	✓
The true cost of the product to the trader is £200.	
The trader suffers a VAT cost of £40.	✓
The trader accounts for output VAT of £40 on its purchase from the manufacturer.	
The member of the public suffers a VAT cost of £40.	

The trader is not VAT-registered. Therefore, it cannot recover input VAT of £40 on its purchase. The true cost of the product to the trader is therefore £240, the trader suffering the VAT of £40.

The trader does not account for VAT as it is not VAT-registered (and in any case this would be input VAT on the purchase, not output VAT).

The member of the public suffers no VAT, as the trader is not registered, so does not charge any VAT on the sale.

Chapter 2 VAT basics

2.1 The correct answer is:

Standard-rated supplies only	
Standard and zero-rated supplies	✓
Zero-rated and exempt supplies	
All three types of supply	

2.2 The correct answer are:

Business	Yes, can reclaim ✓	No, cannot reclaim ✓
Bread Ltd – making only standard-rated supplies	✓	
Soup Ltd – making only exempt supplies		✓
Marmalade Ltd – making only zero-rated supplies	✓	

2.3 The correct answer is:

Cost	✓
£0	
£20	
£100	✓
£120	

A VAT-registered trader making zero-rated supplies can recover all its input VAT, and so the cost of the goods is £100.

2.4 The correct answer is:

	Correct
Jam Ltd cannot register for VAT.	
If Jam Ltd is VAT-registered it will make payments to HMRC.	
If Jam Ltd is VAT-registered it will have repayments from HMRC.	✓

Jam Ltd can recover input tax, but has no output tax (charged at 0%), so will be in a net repayment position.

2.5   The correct answer is:

	True	False
If Bradley's business makes zero-rated supplies, it will be in a VAT repayment position.	✓	
If Bradley makes standard-rated supplies, it will be disadvantageous for non VAT-registered customers.	✓	

If Bradley makes zero-rated supplies, he can recover his input tax but has no output tax (charged at 0%) so will be in a repayment position.

If Bradley makes standard-rated supplies, he will have to charge VAT at 20%. Non VAT-registered customers cannot recover this, and so the goods will be more expensive to them.

2.6   The correct answer is:

	Register now	Monitor and register later
An existing business with a total turnover of £6,350 per month for the last 12 months.		✓
A new business with an expected turnover of £25,000 per month for the next 12 months.		✓
An existing business with a total turnover of £6,000 per month for the last 12 months. A new contract will bring in additional sales of £86,000, in 10 days' time.	✓	

The first business has not exceeded the registration threshold of £85,000 in the last 12 months (£6,350 × 12 = £76,200) so does not have to register yet.

The new business has to register once it has exceeded the threshold in the last 12 months (or since starting to trade). It only has to register on the basis of its **expected** turnover, if it is expected to exceed the threshold in the next 30 days alone. This is not the case.

The existing business has not exceeded the threshold in the last 12 months (£6,000 × 12 = £72,000). However the new contract means it will exceed the threshold in the next 30 days alone, and so has to register now under the future test.

2.7   The correct answer is:

	Can register	Cannot register
Blackberry Ltd – making only zero-rated supplies	✓	
Raspberry Ltd – making standard-rated and zero-rated supplies	✓	
Loganberry Ltd – making only exempt supplies		✓
Gooseberry Ltd – making standard-rated and exempt supplies	✓	

2.8   The correct answer is:

	True	False
Flan Ltd cannot register as it makes only zero-rated supplies.		✓
Flan Ltd is automatically exempt from registering for VAT.		✓
Flan Ltd can register for VAT.	✓	
Flan Ltd can apply to HMRC to be exempt from registration.	✓	

Flan Ltd is able to register for VAT, and must do so if it exceeds the registration threshold, but it is possible to apply to HMRC so that it does not have to register, as it makes only zero-rated supplies.

2.9   The correct answer is:

	Include	Exclude
Standard-rated supplies	✓	
Zero-rated supplies	✓	
Exempt supplies		✓

2.10   The correct answer is:

Taxable turnover in the next	12	months is expected to fall below the deregistration limit.

2.11   The correct answer is:

	✓
£85,000	
£83,000	✓
£150,000	
£1.35 million	

2.12   The correct answer is:

	True	False
The business can apply to HMRC for exception from registration, because the level of taxable supplies was temporary.	✓	

Chapter 3 Inputs and outputs

3.1 The correct answer is:

Invoice number	Net £	VAT £	Gross £
1000325	325.50	65.10	390.60
1000326	452.92	90.58	543.50

Workings

£390.60 × 1/6 = £65.10 so net amount = £390.60 − £65.10 = £325.50

£452.92 × 20% = £90.58 so gross amount = £452.92 + £90.58 = £543.50

3.2 The correct answer is:

Circumstance	Yes, can reclaim ✓	No, cannot reclaim ✓
Input tax incurred entertaining a UK client (meals provided during a meeting)		✓
Input tax incurred on the purchase of a van for use by a furniture repair business	✓	
Input tax incurred providing meals on a training course for an employee	✓	

3.3 The correct answer is:

On the VAT return Dish Ltd must include an amount of	**output**	tax to take account of the private fuel used by salesmen.

Output tax in the form of the fuel scale charge must be included.

3.4 The correct answer is:

	✓
Nil	
£2,840.00	
£2,100.00	✓
£4,940.00	

VAT is irrecoverable on cars purchased with both business and private use.

3.5   The correct answer is:

All input tax can be reclaimed.	
Only input tax relating to standard-rated supplies can be reclaimed.	
All input tax can be reclaimed provided certain *de minimis* tests are met.	✓
Only input tax relating to standard and zero-rated supplies can be reclaimed.	
No input tax can be reclaimed.	

3.6   The correct answer is:

Charlotte must pay output VAT of	**£65.50**

The quarterly fuel scale charge is always stated inclusive of VAT so to calculate the output VAT payable you must multiply by 1/6.

Charlotte may reclaim input VAT of	**£40.00**

In this question we are told the fuel cost is £200.00 exclusive of VAT so to calculate the input VAT Charlotte paid you must multiply by 20%.

3.7   The correct answer is:

This purchase is known as an	**import.**

3.8   The correct answer is:

Because the service is business-to-business, it will be	**zero-rated for VAT.**

3.9   The correct answer is:

Goods exported to non-UK customers must be treated as	**zero-rated.**

3.10 The correct answer is:

	Correct
VAT payable to HMRC of £3,100	
VAT reclaimed from HMRC of £3,100	
Nil net VAT effect	✓

VAT is paid to HMRC at the airport/port and then reclaimed as input tax on the VAT return, so the net effect is the same as a purchase in the UK ie nil net VAT effect.

3.11   The correct answer is:

	✓
As this is a business-to-business supply, the French supplier does not need to charge VAT.	
The UK business will charge itself output tax for the goods on its VAT return and reclaim input tax on the same return.	✓
The UK business will pay output tax to HMRC at the point of entry into the UK and reclaim input tax on the next return.	✓
The French supplier will charge VAT on the goods and the UK business will be able to reclaim the VAT on its next return.	

The first statement is incorrect as this is a supply of goods, not services. The status of the recipient has no impact on the zero-rating of the French export.

The second statement is correct if postponed accounting is used by the UK business.

The third statement is incorrect as this describes the usual position for an import.

The fourth statement is incorrect as it is the UK business (and not the French supplier) which must account for the output tax.

Chapter 4 Accounting for VAT

4.1 The correct answer is:

	Yes	No
Standard-rated supplies	✓	
Zero-rated supplies	✓	
Exempt supplies	✓	

4.2 The correct answer is:

VAT records should usually be retained for	6	year(s).

4.3 The correct answer is:

	Yes	No
Sales daybook	✓	
Purchases daybook		✓
Cash receipts book	✓	
Cash payments book		✓

4.4 The correct answer is:

	Yes	No
Sales daybook		✓
Purchases daybook	✓	
Cash receipts book		✓
Cash payments book	✓	
Sales returns daybook		✓
Purchases returns daybook	✓	

4.5 The correct answer is:

A trader must retain a valid VAT	invoice	in order to reclaim input tax.

4.6 The correct answer is:

	✓
The supplier's name and address	
The date of supply	
Description of the goods/ services	
The total excluding VAT	✓

For each applicable VAT rate the total including VAT is required together with the rates.

4.7   The correct answer is:

Invoice	Valid ✓	Not valid ✓	Missing item(s)
(a)		✓	Invoice number
(b)		✓	Supplier's address
(c)		✓	Supplier's VAT registration number/ Applicable rates of VAT (0% & 20%)
(d)	✓		

Note.

The total value of the supply by Jewels & Co, including VAT, does not exceed £250, so a less detailed invoice is permissible.

The invoice is valid, because it includes all the information which must be shown on a less detailed invoice.

4.8   The correct answer is:

	True	False
The supplier charges VAT at the reduced rate of 5%		✓
The supplier must always calculate and state the amount of VAT to be reverse-charged on the invoice		✓
The customer must be registered under the Construction Industry Scheme	✓	
The customer must be registered for VAT.	✓	

4.9   The correct answer is:

	✓
Sale of goods by a retailer at a VAT inclusive value exceeding £250.	✓
Sale at a VAT inclusive value of less than £250.	
A VAT reverse charge will apply under the Construction Industry Scheme.	
Sale of goods to non-UK customers.	

4.10   The correct answer is:

	✓
Vase Foods will need to implement procedures to ensure the authenticity and integrity of their electronic invoices	✓
HMRC must receive copies of all electronic invoices issued	
Vase foods' customers must agree to receive electronic invoices	✓
Vase foods' customers must settle the invoices via bank transfer	
The file type must enable invoices to be amended (eg Word document)	

4.11   The correct answer is:

	✓
More VAT payable	
Less VAT payable	✓

The credit note will decrease the output tax, and so less VAT will be payable.

4.12   The correct answer is:

	✓
Output tax will increase.	
Output tax will decrease.	
Input tax will increase.	
Input tax will decrease.	✓

4.13   The correct answer is:

	✓
13 August and actual tax point	✓
13 August and basic tax point	
14 August and actual tax point	
14 August and basic tax point	

The basic tax point is 14 August, the date of delivery of the goods, but the invoice date is before this, so the tax point is an actual tax point of 13 August.

4.14   The correct answer is:

	✓
13 August	
15 August	✓
31 August	
15 September	

The basic tax point is 15 August, the date of delivery of the goods, and the invoice is issued more than 14 days later, so this does not create an actual tax point.

4.15 The correct answer is:

Invoice number	Shown on invoice as	
	VAT exclusive £	VAT £
25	198.00	39.60
26 (discounted value)	194.00	38.80
26 (undiscounted value)	200.00	40.00

Working

£200.00 × 97% = 194.00

£194.00 × 20% = £38.80

4.16 The correct answer is:

	✓
Six months must have elapsed since payment was due.	
Output tax has been accounted for and paid.	
Notice must have been received from the customer's liquidators to state that it is insolvent.	✓
The debt must have been written-off in the accounts of Knife Ltd.	

ANSWERS

Chapter 5 The VAT return

5.1   The correct answer is:

VAT-registered traders must usually complete a VAT return every	3	months.

5.2   The correct answer is:

	✓
A VAT payment due to HMRC	
A VAT repayment from HMRC	✓

5.3   The correct answer is:

(a)   **VAT return to 31 May 20X0 submission date**

	✓
30 June 20X0	
7 July 20X0	✓
10 July 20X0	

(b)   **VAT due**

	✓
30 June 20X0	
7 July 20X0	✓
10 July 20X0	

5.4   The correct answer is:

(a)   **VAT return to 31 May 20X0 submission date**

	✓
30 June 20X0	
7 July 20X0	✓
10 July 20X0	

(b)   **VAT due**

	✓
30 June 20X0	
7 July 20X0	
10 July 20X0	✓

5.5 The correct answer is:

(a)

	✓
Input tax reclaimable will be increased and the bad debt VAT will be included in box 4 on the VAT return.	✓
Output tax payable will be decreased and the bad debt VAT will be included as a deduction in box 1 on the VAT return.	

(b)

	✓
Output tax payable will be increased and the fuel scale charge will be included in box 1 on the VAT return.	✓
Input tax reclaimable will be decreased and the fuel scale charge will be included as a deduction in box 4 on the VAT return.	

5.6 The correct answer is:

(a)

The figure for VAT due on imports under postponed accounting is:	£	940.00

£4,700 × 20% = £940.00

(b)

The figure for box 1 of the VAT return is:	£	3,750.00

VAT due in this period on sales and other outputs = £1,800 + £1,010 + £940

(c)

The figure for box 4 of the VAT return is:	£	1,195.00

VAT reclaimed in the period on purchases and other inputs, including imports = £450 − £195 + £940

(d) The correct answer is:

	✓
The flat rate scheme has been applied.	
The VAT software has been set up to apply the cash accounting scheme.	
VAT on imports has yet to be accounted for on the VAT return software.	✓
The VAT software has accounted for VAT on the business's UK sales at the reduced rate.	

5.7   The correct answer is:

	✓
Bad debt relief	✓
Purchases returns	
VAT on imports	✓
Sales returns	

The corrected VAT return should show the following:

Workings		£
Box 1	VAT on sales from the sales daybook	5,900.00
	VAT due on imports (2,140 × 20%)	**428.00**
	Less: VAT on credit notes	(500.00)
		5,828.00
Box 2		**0.00**
Box 3	Total of box 1 and box 2	**5,828.00**
Box 4	VAT on purchases from purchases daybook	2,645.00
	VAT on imports	428.00
	Bad debt relief (720.00 × 1/6)	120.00
	Less: VAT on credit notes	(340.00)
		2,853.00
Box 5	Net VAT due Box 3 minus box 4 £5,828 – £2,853	**2,975.00**
Box 6	Zero-rated credit UK sales	17,000.00
	Standard-rated credit UK sales	29,500.00
	Less: standard-rated credit notes	(2,500.00)
		44,000
Box 7	Standard-rated credit UK purchases	13,225.00
	Imports	2,140.00
	Less: standard-rated credit notes	(1,700.00)
		13,665

Chapter 6 VAT schemes for small businesses

6.1 The correct answer is:

Businesses submit only 1 return each year if they operate the	**annual accounting**	scheme.

To join, taxable supplies in the next 12 months must be below £	**1,350,000**	

6.2 The correct answer is:

A business gets automatic bad debt relief if it operates the	**cash accounting**	scheme.

6.3 The correct answer is:

Harry's VAT payable is calculated as a percentage of the VAT	**inclusive**	turnover.

6.4 The correct answer is:

	✓
She pays some of her VAT by monthly instalments with the balance due by 31 May 20X0.	
She pays some of her VAT by monthly instalments with the balance due by 30 June 20X0.	✓
She pays all of her VAT in a single payment by 31 May 20X0.	
She pays all of her VAT in a single payment by 30 June 20X0.	

6.5 The correct answer is:

	True	False
VAT is accounted for on the basis of cash paid and received rather than on invoices.	✓	
The scheme is advantageous for businesses making only zero-rated supplies.		✓*
Businesses must leave the scheme if taxable supplies in the previous 12 months exceed £1,350,000.		✓**

* Input tax is generally reclaimed later under the cash accounting scheme, so this is not advantageous

** The limit for leaving is £1,600,000

6.6 The correct answer is:

	True	False
Businesses issue normal VAT invoices to customers.	✓	
VAT is paid in instalments.		✓
The flat rate percentage applied always depends on the type of business.		✓*
Less VAT may be payable by Jack as a result of operating the scheme.	✓	

* limited cost traders use a flat rate of 16.5% irrespective of the type of business

6.7   The correct answer is:

		✓
Yes, because output VAT would be paid later and input VAT would be reclaimed at the same time or earlier.		✓
No, because input VAT would be reclaimed later and output VAT would be paid at the same time or earlier.		

6.8   The correct answer is:

	✓
£5,544.00	
£4,950.00	
£4,944.00	✓
£4,704.00	

Gross total turnover is £(18,000 × 1.2 + 12,000) = £33,600

£33,600 × 16.5% (limited cost trader %) = £5,544

Input tax recoverable on fixed assets costing over £2,000 = 20% × £3,000 = £600

VAT payable is therefore £(5,544-600) = £4,944.00

Chapter 7 Payroll systems

7.1 The correct answer is:

Mr Pick must register with HMRC for payroll taxes between **28 June 2022** and **27 August 2022**.

Registration must be prior to, but not more than two months prior to the first planned payment.

7.2 The correct answers are:

	True	False
HMRC require employers to keep records of employees' leave and sickness absence	✓	
Payroll records for the tax year 2021/22 must be kept until 5 April 2028		✓
Employee pay records are personal data and as such their storage is governed by GDPR	✓	
HMRC may make an unannounced visit to an employer's premises to inspect payroll records		✓

Payroll records for 2021/22 are required to be kept until 5 April 2025 (three years). HMRC are required to give notice to an employer prior to visiting their premises.

7.3 (a) Mrs String's gross pay for June 2021 is **£2,000**

(b) Mrs String's net pay for June 2021 is **£1,440**

(c) Neck Ltd must pay **£510** to HMRC in respect of Mrs String's pay for the month of June 2021, on or before **22/7/2021**

7.4 The correct answers are:

	True	False
Payroll software is used to provide information to HMRC under Real Time Information (RTI).	✓	
Payroll software can calculate statutory maternity pay.	✓	
All payroll software that is tested and approved by HRMC will be suitable for any business.		✓
Once installed, payroll software will never need to be updated.		✓

7.5 The correct answers are:

Form	Function
Full Payment Submission (FPS)	Return showing pay and deductions for each employee on a specific payment date
P11D	End of year summary of taxable benefits
P45	Details of employee leaving
P60	End of year summary of pay and deductions

7.6 (a) The payment was made on time

(b) The forms were provided late

The deadline for electronic payment of Class 1A NIC is 22nd July after the end of the tax year. The deadline for the P11D forms to be provided to employees is 6 July.

7.7 A Full Payment Submission (FPS) form must be filed with HMRC every **time employees are paid**

An Employer Payment Summary (EPS) must be filed every **month** where no employees are paid.

7.8

	£
Gross pay per P60 in 2021/22	35,000
PAYE	−4486
Employee's national insurance contributions	−3051.84
Student loan deductions	−156.00
Take-home (net) pay	27,306.16

Chapter 8 VAT and PAYE Administration

8.1 The correct answer is:

	✓
More than the error correction reporting threshold, but not deliberate	
Less than the error correction reporting threshold and not deliberate	✓
More than the error correction reporting threshold and was deliberate	
Less than the error correction reporting threshold, but was deliberate	

8.2 The correct answer is:

	True	False
Amy can adjust this on her next return.		✓
Amy cannot adjust this error on her next return and will be liable for a penalty.		✓

Amy cannot adjust this error on her next return but there will not be a penalty as it was not careless or deliberate.

8.3 The correct answer is:

	✓
No – not shown on the return	
Yes – shown in box 1	
Yes – shown in box 4	✓

It is shown as an increase in the input tax at box 4 on the VAT return.

8.4 The correct answer is:

	✓
No action will be taken by HMRC.	
HMRC will issue a surcharge liability notice.	✓
HMRC will issue a surcharge liability notice and charge a penalty.	
HMRC charge a penalty only.	

8.5 The correct answer is:

A business has a requirement to retain VAT records for	**six**	years.

8.6 The correct answers are:

	✓
A late filing penalty of £100	
A late filing penalty of £200.	✓
A late payment penalty of 1%.	
A penalty of up to 70% of underpaid tax.	✓

The late filing penalty is £200 as Rachel has between 10–49 employees. No late payment penalty arises as the tax was paid before 22 March 20X1. As Rachel deliberately omitted taxable income (the cash bonuses) from the payroll software, PAYE and NIC will have been underpaid and a maximum penalty of 70% of potential lost revenue (PLR) can apply. There is no evidence of Rachel taking steps to conceal the error.

8.7 The correct answer is:

	✓
True	
False	✓

Tax avoidance is a way of trying to legally reduce your tax burden, whereas tax evasion is illegal and consists of seeking to pay too little tax by deliberately misleading HMRC.

8.8 The correct answer is:

To: **Howard** (1)

From: **AN Accountant** (2)

Date: **1 June 20X0** (3)

Subject: **VAT deregistration** (4)

Please be advised that the current level of your business turnover is such that you are able to VAT **deregister.** (5) As you will no longer need to charge **output** (6) VAT to your customers, there are two options open to you.

1. Your selling prices can decrease to the VAT-exclusive amount

    As a result your profits will **stay the same.** (7) At the same time your customer will have **a lower** (8) cost.

2. Your selling prices can stay at the same VAT-inclusive amount

    As a result your profits will **increase.** (9) At the same time your customer will have **the same** (10) cost.

    If you wish to discuss this further please feel free to make an appointment.

    Kind regards

8.9   The correct answer is:

ABC & Co
2 Smith Street
London
W1 2DE

1 October 20X0

Mr Jones
Unit 1 Alias Industrial Estate
Chelmsford
Essex
CM2 3FG

Dear | **Mr Jones** |

| **Annual accounting scheme** |

Further to our telephone conversation of today, I have set out below the details relating to the annual accounting scheme.

Your business can join the annual accounting scheme if the value of its taxable supplies | **excluding** | VAT, in the forthcoming | **12** | months does not exceed £ | **1,350,000.** |

Under this scheme the business usually makes | **nine** | equal monthly instalments. Each of these instalments is | **1/10** | of the prior year VAT liability. The first payment is due at the | **end** | of the | **fourth** | month of the accounting period.

The balancing payment and the VAT return will be sent to HMRC within | **two months** | of the end of the accounting period.

I hope that this has clarified the position. If you wish to discuss this further please do not hesitate to contact me.

Yours sincerely

AAT AQ2022 ASSESSMENT

Tax Processes for Businesses

Students should attempt the AAT practice assessments on the AAT's Lifelong Learning portal prior to taking the actual assessment.

BPP PRACTICE ASSESSMENT 1

Tax Processes for Businesses FA 2021

Time allowed: 1 hour and 30 minutes

Tax Processes for Businesses (TPFB)
BPP practice assessment 1

Task 1 (9 marks)

Joseph makes zero-rated supplies and Julie makes standard-rated supplies. Both are considering voluntarily registering for VAT. Julie's customers are mostly VAT-registered themselves.

(a)   **Identify whether the following statements are true or false.**

TICK ONE BOX per statement.

	True	False
Joseph will be in a repayment position if he voluntarily registers		
Julie's customers will not suffer the impact of her charging VAT unless they are not VAT-registered		
Joseph will be required to make monthly returns if he voluntarily registers		
Both traders will be required to use Making Tax Digital to file their VAT returns if they voluntarily register		

Clover Ltd has been trading for 12 months. You have extracted the following information in relation to the company.

Turnover	VAT excl £
Standard-rated	60,000
Zero-rated	18,000
Exempt	8,000

(b)   **Identify whether the following statement is true or false.**

(Assuming Clover Ltd was not VAT-registered from starting to trade)

	True	False
Clover Ltd must VAT register as total turnover exceeds £85,000.		

Igor has been trading for many years and makes standard-rated supplies. He is in the flat rate scheme. The flat rate percentage that he must use is 10.5%.

In the latest quarter, Igor had total turnover of £9,000 excluding VAT. He also had VAT-exclusive purchases of £2,000.

(c)   (i)   **Identify which ONE of the following is the output tax figure to be included in Igor's VAT return.**

	✓
£945.00	
£1,134.00	
£882.00	

(ii) In this quarter, would Igor have more or less VAT to pay to HMRC if he was not in the flat rate scheme?

	✓
More VAT payable if not in the flat rate scheme	
Less VAT payable if not in the flat rate scheme	

Task 2 (8 marks)

Adam is a VAT-registered trader making standard-rated supplies. He does not use the cash accounting scheme. On 19 March 20X0 he received an order from a customer together with a 10% deposit including VAT of £40. The goods were sent out to the customer on 22 March 20X0. An invoice was sent out on 1 April 20X0 that included VAT of £400. The customer paid the balance of the invoice (including VAT of £360) on 30 April 20X0.

Calculate the amount of output tax to be included on Adam's VAT return to:

(a) (i) **31 March 20X0**

TICK ONE BOX

	✓
Nil	
£40	
£360	
£400	

(ii) **30 June 20X0**

TICK ONE BOX

	✓
Nil	
£40	
£360	
£400	

A manufacturer supplies a reduced-rate item at a VAT inclusive price of £1,575.

(b) (i) **How much output tax should the manufacturer include in its VAT account for this supply?**

£	

(ii) **Assuming the customer is registered for VAT and making wholly taxable supplies, what will be the cost to their business of the purchase of the goods?**

£	

A trader sells goods with a list price of £2000 plus VAT at the standard rate but offers a settlement discount of 5% for payment within 30 days. The customer pays after 45 days. The trader's original invoice showed both the full and discounted amounts.

(c) (i) **What action does the trader now need to take?**

TICK ONE BOX

	✓
Re-issue an invoice for the full price	
Issue an invoice for the amount of the discount	
No action is required	
Issue a credit note for the discount	

(ii) **Identify which THREE of the following items must also be included on the trader's invoice for it to be valid for VAT purposes**

TICK 3 BOXES

	✓
An invoice number	
The customer's VAT registration number	
The customer's name and address	
The credit period offered	
Instructions to the customer about recoverability of input VAT	

Task 3 (12 marks)

A VAT-registered business makes a mixture of exempt and taxable supplies.

(a) **Which ONE of the following statements is/are true?**

	✓
Only the input tax relating to taxable supplies is recoverable, in all circumstances.	
All input tax is recoverable if certain *de minimis* tests are satisfied.	
No input tax is recoverable.	
All input tax is recoverable as no supplies are outside the scope of VAT.	

Jagger Ltd is not permitted to register for VAT and all of its purchases must be included in its statement of profit or loss at their VAT-inclusive price.

(b) **What type of supplies does Jagger Ltd make?**

	✓
Standard rated	
Reduced rated	
Zero rated	
Exempt	

Moon Plc is a VAT-registered company making wholly taxable supplies. It provides its employees with company cars for both business and private use, and also pays for all fuel in relation to these cars.

(c) **Which TWO of the following are acceptable options for Moon Plc in relation to the VAT on fuel for private motoring?**

	✓
Reclaim no input VAT on any fuel	
Reclaim all input VAT on fuel as the business makes wholly taxable supplies	
Approximate a split of business and private mileage based on prior experience, then reclaim the input VAT relating to the approximate business proportion	
Reclaim all input VAT on all fuel, but add the relevant fuel scale charge to output VAT	

(d) You have extracted the following information from the accounting records of a VAT-registered client.

For each item of expenditure:

(i) Identify whether the input tax can be recovered or is blocked

(ii) Calculate the amount of input tax that can be recovered. Round down figures to the nearest penny. If your answer is zero, enter '0.00'.

Detail	Recover input tax ✓	Blocked input tax ✓	Input tax that can be recovered £
Car (for use by salesman) costing £16,800 inclusive of VAT at the standard rate			
Hotels (for sales reps while on business) costing £2,890 inclusive of VAT at the standard rate			
UK client lunches costing £558 inclusive of VAT at the standard rate			
Entertaining overseas clients at a cost of £500 exclusive of VAT at the standard rate			

Task 4 (8 marks)

This task is about preparing, calculating and adjusting information for VAT returns.

Reed Ltd prepares VAT returns for the quarters ending 31 March, 30 June, 30 September, and 31 December and does not use a specialist scheme.

You work for a firm of accountants and are assisting with the preparation of the VAT return for Reed Ltd for the quarter ended 31 December 2021.

Reed Ltd has turnover of £2,000,000 and has discovered an error in its VAT return for the quarter ended 31 June 2021 that has resulted in an underpayment of £12,500.

(a)   **What is the correct action to take?**

	✓
Ignore the error	
Correct the error on the next VAT return	
Disclose the error separately through a Form 652	

The correct VAT payable by Reed Ltd for the quarter ended 31 December 2021 is shown on the VAT return software as £60,400.00. However, on reviewing the figures within Reed Ltd's accounting software, you find that the VAT account at the end of this period shows a balance of £70,400.00.

(b)   **Which ONE of the following statements could explain the difference?**

	✓
The VAT payment for the previous period of £5,000.00 was not posted to the VAT account.	
The VAT payment for the previous period of £5,000.00 was posted to the wrong side of the VAT account.	

The financial controller of Reed Ltd has contacted you, advising that some year-end transactions had yet to be entered in the accounting records provided to you, and that they may impact on the VAT payable for the quarter ended 31 December 2021.

(c)   **Calculate the changes that need to be made to the figures for output tax and input tax for each transaction.** Round down your answers to the nearest penny. If there is no change enter 0.00.

Transaction	Output tax £	Input tax £
23 December 2021 Write-off of a bad debt that was due for payment in April 2021. The amount written off was £480 inclusive of VAT at the standard rate.		
24 December 2021 Accrual for legal advice not yet invoiced by the supplier, total amount accrued £1,500 inclusive of VAT at the standard rate.		
29 December 20X1 Receipt of an invoice relating to the purchase by Reed Ltd of a new machine costing £120,000 inclusive of VAT.		
30 December 2021 Delivery to Reed Ltd of goods imported from Germany, accompanied by an invoice from the German supplier for £12,000. Reed Ltd accounts for input VAT on imports via postponed accounting.		

Reed Ltd will be importing goods for the first time in the quarter ended 31 March 2022. The directors have asked you to explain the difference between accounting for VAT at the border compared to postponed accounting.

(d) **Identify which of the following statements is true in relation to postponed accounting.**

	✓
Postponed accounting will result in a lower overall VAT liability than accounting for VAT at the border	
Postponed accounting requires fewer entries on Reed Ltd's VAT return	
VAT on the import of goods under postponed accounting is always at a rate of 20%	
Postponed accounting will improve Reed Ltd's cash flow position	

Task 5 (12 marks)

This task is about verifying VAT returns.

Company A uses Making Tax Digital-compliant VAT return preparation software which is separate from its accounting systems.

You work for Company A as an assistant in the accounts department and your manager has asked you to review the draft VAT return for the period ended 31 December 20X0 that was generated from the software and to reconcile it to the company's accounting records.

The following accounts have been extracted from Company A's accounting systems for quarter ended 31 December 20X0.

Sales daybook summary

	Zero-rated sales £	Standard-rated sales £	VAT £	Total £
UK sales	12,000.00	7,000.00	1,400.00	20,400.00

Purchases daybook summary

	Zero-rated purchases £	Standard-rated purchases £	VAT £	Total £
UK purchases/expenses	2,500.00	7,200.00	1,440.00	11,140.00

Purchases returns daybook summary

	Standard-rated purchases £	VAT £	Total £
UK purchases	2,300.00	460.00	2,760.00

In December 20X0 two debts (on standard-rated sales) were written off as irrecoverable (bad) in Company A's accounting records. The first debt was for £758 on an invoice dated 15 March 20X0; the second was for £622 with an invoice dated 23 June 20X0. Company A's payment terms are strictly 30 days from date of invoice. Both figures are stated inclusive of VAT.

(a) (i) **When reconciling the above information to the VAT return software, which boxes should contain the following figures?**

Transactions	Box 1 ✓	Box 4 ✓
VAT on standard-rated sales		
VAT on standard-rated purchases		
VAT on purchases returns		
VAT bad debt relief		

(ii) **Indicate whether the following statements are true or false in relation to the sales and purchases information to be entered in Boxes 6 and 7 of the VAT return**

	True ✓	False ✓
Sales are entered in Box 6, and will include zero-rated sales		
Figures in Boxes 6 and 7 are stated inclusive of VAT		

(iii) **Calculate the figure to be reclaimed for bad debt relief in the quarter ended 31/12/X0.**

The figure to be reclaimed for bad debt relief is:	£	

(iv) **Complete the following sentence:**

If bad debt relief were claimed on both of the debts written off in the quarter, the

error would result in the output VAT for the quarter being [▼] and

the input VAT recoverable for the quarter being [▼]

Picklist:

understated
overstated
correct

The Box 1 figure from the VAT return software shows output VAT of £2,000.

(b) (i) **Which of the following reasons would fully explain the difference between this figure and the VAT of £1,400 per the sales day book?**

	✓
The VAT return software incorrectly applying the standard rate of VAT to all sales	
The VAT return software incorrectly applying the reduced rate of VAT to zero-rated sales	
VAT on imports with a VAT exclusive cost of £3,600 being omitted from the accounting records	
The VAT return software has applied the flat rate scheme with a flat rate percentage of 10%	

(ii)   What is the appropriate action for you to take in respect of this discrepancy?

	✓
Amend the settings within the VAT software and submit the VAT return	
Amend the accounting systems by deleting certain sales transactions	
Take no action and submit the VAT return	
Amend the settings within the VAT software and ask your manager to review the revised VAT return before its submission	

Task 6 (11 marks)

Company A is a growing business that has been registered for VAT for many years and uses the cash accounting scheme. The financial controller, who was responsible for all previous VAT returns, has recently left the company and the directors are concerned about the company's VAT compliance history.

Company A typically offers its customers 60 days' credit and receives 30 days' credit from suppliers. Taxable supplies made by Company A are currently £1.2 million per year.

(a)   (i)   Identify whether the following statements are true or false.

TICK ONE BOX PER STATEMENT

	True	False
If Company A submits an inaccurate VAT return but tells HMRC of the inaccuracy as soon as possible, this may reduce the possible penalty		
Tax evasion is illegal and may lead to fines and imprisonment		
A careless underpayment of VAT carries a maximum penalty of 30% of the underpaid tax		

(ii)   Select TWO statements which are correct in relation to Company A's use of the cash accounting scheme.

	✓
If Company A's turnover exceeds £1.6 million, it must exit the scheme	
Leaving the cash accounting scheme will result in more VAT being payable in total	
Leaving the cash accounting scheme will mean that Company A has to pay its VAT earlier than it currently does	
Leaving the cash accounting scheme will mean that Company A must file its VAT returns earlier	

(b) The directors of Company A are worried that the financial controller may not have kept the required VAT records.

(i) **Identify which of the following records Company A would be required to keep in relation to the calculation of its VAT liability for the quarter ended 30 September 2021.**

	Required ✓	Not required ✓
Cash received from credit customers in July 2021		
Invoices received from suppliers in September 2021, with credit terms of 30 days		
Records of goods imported from Spain in August 2021		
Refunds paid to credit customers in relation to sales made in June 2021		

(ii) **Complete the following statement concerning retention of VAT records:**

All Company A's VAT records [▼] be kept electronically. Failure to retain the correct VAT records for a return period may result in a penalty of

[▼]

Picklist:

(1) may
    must
    cannot

(2) £100
    £3,000
    100% of the VAT liability

Task 7

(a) Match the following facts with the payroll forms they relate to (more than one form may be selected) **(5 marks)**

	Payslip ✓	P45 ✓	P60 ✓	P11D ✓	FPS ✓	EPS ✓
Filed with HMRC under RTI						
Must show the number of hours an employee works, if the pay varies depending on time worked						
Provided to employees by 31 May following the end of each tax year						
Provided to employees by 6 July following the end of each tax year						
Gives details about employees who have left						
Copy provided to both HMRC and the employee						

(b)   JK Kitchens Ltd employs 10 members of staff, each paid monthly. It submits its FPS return late for the month of September and this is the second time that it has submitted it late this year.

(i)   What is the penalty in relation to the late filing of FPS return?   £ [   ]

The associated PAYE liability of £8,450 was also paid one month late. The company had previously made late payments in May, June, July and August this year.

(ii)   What is the penalty in relation to the late payment of PAYE?

£ [   ]

(c)   John is employed by Jamie's gym. He is provided with his P60 showing the following details:

Pay and Income Tax details

	Pay		Tax deducted	
	£	p	£	p
In previous employment(s)		0		0
In this employment		32,940.00		4,074.00
Total for year		32,940.00		4,074.00

National Insurance contributions in this employment

NIC table letter	Earnings at the Lower Earnings Limit (LEL) (where earnings are equal to or exceed the LEL) £	Earnings above the LEL, up to and including the Primary Threshold (PT) £	Earnings above the PT, up to and including the Upper Earnings Limit (UEL) £	Employee's contributions due on all earnings above the PT £ p
A	6,240	3,328	23,372	2,804.64

(i)   By what date must Jamie's gym provide John with his P60 for 2021/22? [DD/MM/YYYY] **(1 mark)**

(ii)   Which THREE of the following other details must be shown on the P60? **(3 marks)**

	✓
tax code	
national insurance number	
employee's address	
employer's address	
Taxable benefits	
Employer's NIC	

(iii)   What is John's net pay for the year? **(1 mark)**

Task 8 (8 marks)

You work for a VAT-registered company and have just completed the VAT return via Making Tax Digital software for the quarter ended 31 March 2021. The VAT return showed an amount of £2,800.00 in Box 1 and in Box 3, and an amount of £800.00 in Box 4.

(a) **Complete the memo to the financial controller regarding the payment of VAT for this quarter.**

MEMO	
To:	Financial Controller
From:	An Accountant
Subject:	VAT payment for the quarter ended 31 March 2021
Date:	14 April 2021

The VAT [▼] (1) is [▼] (2). We [▼] (3) this by [▼] (4).

Picklist:

(1) payable
    repayable

(2) £2,800.00
    £800.00
    £2,000.00

(3) must pay
    will receive

(4) 30 April 2021
    7 May 2021

The company's managing director is interested in the benefits of using the annual accounting scheme and has asked you to prepare a short report for him containing relevant information.

(b) (i) **Which TWO of the following sources of information would you use to assist you in preparing the report?**

TICK TWO:

	✓
Calling the HMRC VAT helpline	
The company's accounts for the previous year	
Information contained on the gov.uk website	
Discussion with your father-in-law, who is a retired accountant.	

(ii)   If you determine that the company is eligible for, and would benefit from, the annual accounting scheme, what action should you take?

	✓
Apply for the scheme on behalf of the company	
Recommend the company applies for the scheme in your report to the managing director	
Take no action as it is not your responsibility to do so	
Discuss the issue at college, in order to inform fellow students of the benefits for their employers	

(iii)   If the company decides to enter the annual accounting scheme, on what day will the VAT return for the year ended 31 December 2022 be due?

	✓
7 February 2023	
28 February 2023	
7 March 2023	
31 December 2024	

BPP PRACTICE ASSESSMENT 1

Tax Processes for Businesses FA 2021

ANSWERS

Tax Processes for Businesses (TPFB)
BPP practice assessment 1

Task 1

(a)

	True	False
Joseph will be in a repayment position if he voluntarily registers	✓	
Julie's customers will not suffer the impact of her charging VAT unless they are not VAT-registered	✓	
Joseph will be required to make monthly returns if he voluntarily registers		✓
Both traders will be required to use Making Tax Digital to file their VAT returns if they voluntarily register		✓

Monthly returns are optional for repayment traders such as Joseph. As both traders' taxable supplies are below the VAT registration threshold, use of Making Tax Digital is voluntary.

(b)

	True	False
Clover Ltd must VAT register as total turnover exceeds £85,000.		✓

Only taxable turnover is considered when determining whether the threshold has been exceeded. Taxable turnover is £78,000.

(c) (i)

	✓
£945.00	
£1,134.00	✓
£882.00	

(£9,000 × 120%) × 10.5% = £1,134.00

(ii)

	✓
More VAT payable if not in the flat rate scheme	✓
Less VAT payable if not in the flat rate scheme	

If not in the flat rate scheme Igor's VAT payable would be:

		£
Output tax	£9,000 × 20%	1,800.00
Input tax	£2,000 × 20%	(400.00)
		1,400.00

As this is more than £1,134.00 Igor would have more VAT payable.

Task 2

(a) (i) **31 March 20X0**

	✓
Nil	
£40	✓
£360	
£400	

(ii) **30 June 20X0**

	✓
Nil	
£40	
£360	✓
£400	

(b) (i)

£	75.00

£1,575 × 5/105

(ii)

£	1,500.00

(c) (i)

	✓
Re-issue an invoice for the full price	
Issue an invoice for the amount of the discount	
No action is required	✓
Issue a credit note for the discount	

(ii)

	✓
An invoice number	✓
The customer's VAT registration number	
The customer's name and address	✓
The credit period offered	
Instructions to the customer about recoverability of input VAT	✓

Task 3

(a)

	✓
Only the input tax relating to taxable supplies is recoverable, in all circumstances.	
All input tax is recoverable if certain *de minimis* tests are satisfied.	✓
No input tax is recoverable.	
All input tax is recoverable as no supplies are outside the scope of VAT.	

(b)

	✓
Standard rated	
Reduced rated	
Zero rated	
Exempt	✓

(c)

	✓
Reclaim no input VAT on any fuel	✓
Reclaim all input VAT on fuel as the business makes wholly taxable supplies	
Approximate a split of business and private mileage based on prior experience, then reclaim the input VAT relating to the approximate business proportion	
Reclaim all input VAT on all fuel, but add the relevant fuel scale charge to output VAT	✓

(d)

Detail	Recover input tax ✓	Blocked input tax ✓	Input tax that can be recovered £
Car (for use by salesman) costing £16,800 inclusive of VAT at the standard rate		✓	0.00
Hotels (for sales reps while on business) costing £2,890 inclusive of VAT at the standard rate	✓		£481.66
UK client lunches costing £558 inclusive of VAT at the standard rate		✓	0.00
Entertaining overseas clients at a cost of £500 exclusive of VAT at the standard rate	✓		100.00

Task 4

(a)

	✓
Ignore the error	
Correct the error on the next VAT return	✓
Disclose the error separately through a Form 652	

The error is less than the higher of £10,000 or 1% of turnover (£20,000), and can therefore be corrected by adjusting the next VAT return.

(b)

	✓
The VAT payment for the previous period of £5,000.00 was not posted to the VAT account.	
The VAT payment for the previous period of £5,000.00 was posted to the wrong side of the VAT account.	✓

(c)

Transaction	Output tax £	Input tax £
23 December 2021 Write-off of a bad debt that was due for payment in April 2021. The amount written off was £480 inclusive of VAT at the standard rate.	0.00	80.00
24 December 2021 Accrual for legal advice not yet invoiced by the supplier, total amount accrued £1,500 inclusive of VAT at the standard rate.	0.00	0.00
29 December 20X1 Receipt of an invoice relating to the purchase by Reed Ltd of a new machine costing £120,000 inclusive of VAT.	0.00	20,000.00
30 December 2021 Delivery to Reed Ltd of goods imported from Germany, accompanied by an invoice from the German supplier for £12,000. Reed Ltd accounts for input VAT on imports via postponed accounting.	2,000.00	2,000.00

(d)

	✓
Postponed accounting will result in a lower overall VAT liability than accounting for VAT at the border	
Postponed accounting requires fewer entries on Reed Ltd's VAT return	
VAT on the import of goods under postponed accounting is always at a rate of 20%	
Postponed accounting will improve Reed Ltd's cash flow position	✓

Task 5

(a) (i)

Transactions	Box 1 ✓	Box 4 ✓
VAT on standard-rated sales	✓	
VAT on standard-rated purchases		✓
VAT on purchases returns		✓
VAT bad debt relief		✓

(ii)

	True ✓	False ✓
Sales are entered in Box 6, and will include zero-rated sales	✓	
Figures in Boxes 6 and 7 are stated inclusive of VAT		✓

(iii)

The figure to be reclaimed for bad debt relief is:	£	126.33

£758 × 1/6 = £126.33

Only the first bad debt (dated 15 March 20X0) is more than six months overdue as at 31 December 20X0. Input VAT may not be recovered on the invoice dated 23 June 20X0 as it will not be six months overdue until 23 January 20X1.

(iv) If bad debt relief were claimed on both of the debts written off in the quarter, the error would result in the output VAT for the quarter being **correct** and the input VAT recoverable for the quarter being **overstated**

(b) (i)

	✓
The VAT return software incorrectly applying the standard rate of VAT to all sales	
The VAT return software incorrectly applying the reduced rate of VAT to zero-rated sales	✓
VAT on imports with a VAT exclusive cost of £3,600 being omitted from the accounting records	
The VAT return software has applied the flat rate scheme with a flat rate percentage of 10%	

Output VAT would be (£12,000 × 5%) = £600 higher on the VAT return software with reduced-rate applying to zero-rated sales.

(ii)

	✓
Amend the settings within the VAT software and submit the VAT return	
Amend the accounting systems by deleting certain sales transactions	
Take no action and submit the VAT return	
Amend the settings within the VAT software and ask your manager to review the revised VAT return before its submission.	✓

Task 6

(a) (i)

	True	False
If Company A submits an inaccurate VAT return but tells HMRC of the inaccuracy as soon as possible, this may reduce the possible penalty	✓	
Tax evasion is illegal and may lead to fines and imprisonment	✓	
A careless underpayment of VAT carries a maximum penalty of 30% of the underpaid tax	✓	

(ii)

		✓
If Company A's turnover exceeds £1.6 million, it must exit the scheme		✓
Leaving the cash accounting scheme will result in more VAT being payable in total		
Leaving the cash accounting scheme will mean that Company A has to pay its VAT earlier than it currently does		✓
Leaving the cash accounting scheme will mean that Company A must file its VAT returns earlier		

(b) (i)

	Required ✓	Not required ✓
Cash received from credit customers in July 2021	✓	
Invoices received from suppliers in September 2021, with credit terms of 30 days		✓
Records of goods imported from Spain in August 2021	✓	
Refunds paid to credit customers in relation to sales made in June 2021	✓	

Company A uses the cash accounting scheme, so invoices from suppliers in September will affect the VAT return for the quarter ended 31 December 2021

(ii) All Company A's VAT records **may** be kept electronically. Failure to retain the correct VAT records for a return period may result in a penalty of **£3,000**

Task 7

(a)

	Payslip ✓	P45 ✓	P60 ✓	P11D ✓	FPS ✓	EPS ✓
Filed with HMRC under RTI					✓	✓
Must show the number of hours an employee works, if the pay varies depending on time worked	✓					
Provided to employees by 31 May following the end of each tax year			✓			
Provided to employees by 6 July following the end of each tax year				✓		
Gives details about employees who have left		✓			✓	
Copy provided to both HMRC and the employee		✓	✓	✓		

(b) (i)   **£200**

(ii) $1\% \times £8{,}450 = $ **£84.50**

The first failure to pay in a tax year does not count as a default, so there were 3 previous defaults making the percentage 1%.

(c) (i)   **31/05/2022**

(ii)

	✓
tax code	✓
national insurance number	✓
employee's address	
employer's address	✓
Taxable benefits	
Employer's NIC	

(iii)   £32,940 − £4,074 − £2,804.64 = £26,061.36

ANSWERS

Task 8

(a)

MEMO

To: Financial Controller

From: An Accountant

Subject: VAT payment for the quarter ended 31 March 20X1

Date: 14 April 2021

The VAT | payable | is | £2,000.00 |. We | must pay | this by | 7 May 20X1. |

(b) (i)

	✓
Calling the HMRC VAT helpline	
The company's accounts for the previous year	✓
Information contained on the gov.uk website	✓
Discussion with your father-in-law, who is a retired accountant.	

(ii)

	✓
Apply for the scheme on behalf of the company	
Recommend the company applies for the scheme in your report to the managing director	✓
Take no action as it is not your responsibility to do so	
Discuss the issue at college, in order to inform fellow students of the benefits for their employers	

(iii)

	✓
7 February 2023	
28 February 2023	✓
7 March 2023	
31 December 2024	

BPP PRACTICE ASSESSMENT 2

Tax Processes for Businesses FA 2021

Time allowed: 1 hour and 30 minutes

Tax Processes for Businesses (TPFB)
BPP practice assessment 2

Task 1 (8 marks)

(a) **Which of the following identifies HMRC's primary role in relation to VAT?**

	✓
Assisting overseas businesses in complying with UK VAT regulations	
The collection and administration of VAT from UK registered businesses	
The calculation of VAT liabilities for UK registered businesses	
Creation of UK VAT law	

(b) Match the statements below to the correct type of supply

Zero-rated supplies	
Standard-rated supplies	
Exempt supplies	
Supplies outside the scope of VAT	

Picklist:

Traders making only this type of supply are not permitted to register for VAT

These supplies have no effect on the VAT calculation

Traders making this type of supply usually generate refunds of input tax

The rate of tax on this type of supply is 20%

John, a trader, failed to register for VAT on time due to carelessness, and immediately informed HMRC as soon as he became aware of his error. Standard-rated sales invoiced in the six months since registration became effective have totalled £75,000. John has approached the customers but they have refused to pay the VAT.

(c) (i) **What amount of VAT will John have to pay to HMRC in respect of these sales?**

£ [   ]

(ii) Complete the following sentence:

John's penalty for late registration will be between [▼] and

[▼] of the underpaid VAT

Picklist:

0
10
20
30
70
100

Task 2 (8 marks)

(a) Identify whether the following statement is true or false.

	True	False
The basic tax point for goods is when an order is received.		

(b) Identify whether the following statements in relation to VAT invoices are true or false.

TICK ONE BOX

	True	False
A VAT invoice must include certain details including the supplier's VAT registration number, the total VAT payable and a description of the goods supplied.		
A less detailed invoice may be issued if the VAT inclusive proceeds are less than £150.		
Modified invoices are made for all sales with a value of less than £250 and must include the total VAT-inclusive selling price.		

(c) Insert the missing VAT figures in the unshaded boxes of the table below.

Supply	Net £	VAT £	Gross £
Standard rated	AUTOSUM		270.60
Standard rated	260.00		AUTOSUM
Reduced rate	AUTOSUM		682.50
Zero rate	500.00		AUTOSUM

Task 3 (12 marks)

This task is about the recovery of input tax.

(a) Which ONE of the following statements is TRUE about a VAT-registered company making both standard-rated and exempt supplies?

	✓
No input VAT can be recovered.	
All input VAT can always be recovered because the company makes some taxable supplies.	
All input VAT can be recovered, provided certain de minimis limits are not exceeded.	

Xavier has a quarter ended 31 December 20X0. His normal payment terms are one calendar month after invoice date. He does not operate any special VAT schemes. All supplies are standard-rated.

(b) **For each bad debt identified:**

(i)   Identify whether the debt is eligible for bad debt relief

(ii)   calculate the amount of bad debt relief available. Round down figures to the nearest penny.

Bad debt	Eligible for bad debt relief ✓	Not eligible for bad debt relief ✓	Amount of bad debt relief available £
Moraira Ltd owes £3,000 from an invoice issued on 2 January 20X0. Xavier believes that the amount will be paid in full and so it has not been written-off in the accounts.			
Calpe Ltd owes £2,000 from an invoice issued on 15 May 20X0. Xavier does not expect that the amount will be paid and so it has been written-off in the accounts.			

Xavier has incurred the motor expenses shown below (all items exclusive of VAT at the standard rate) in the quarter ended 31 December 20X1. His detailed mileage records for his own car show that he drove 2,000 miles in the quarter, of which 1,500 were for business journeys. He will use these records where relevant to reclaim his input VAT.

(c) For each expense listed:

(i)   Identify whether the input tax incurred by Xavier can be recovered, is blocked, or can be partly recovered.

(ii)   Calculate the amount of input tax which can be recovered. Round down figures to the nearest penny. If your answer is zero, enter '0.00'.

Expense	Recover input tax ✓	Blocked input tax ✓	Partly blocked input tax ✓	Amount of VAT recoverable £
Xavier purchased a car for his own use (see above), costing £14,000				
Xavier paid fuels costs of £470 in the quarter in respect of his own car				
Xavier purchased a car costing £9,000 for the use of his employees, for business journeys only. The car is kept at the business' premises overnight				

Task 4 (8 marks)

A business has completed its VAT return using Making Tax Digital software, which shows a correct amount of £5,600.00 owing to HMRC. The VAT account at the end of the same period shows a liability of £8,000.00.

(a) Which ONE of the following could explain this difference?

	✓
The VAT payment for the previous period of £2,400 has not been entered in the VAT account.	
The VAT payment for the previous period of £2,400 has been entered twice in the VAT account.	

Joseph Marselus accidentally left out a couple of invoices from his last VAT return.

- Invoice 1 was for £3,400.00 (VAT-exclusive) to a customer
- Invoice 2 was for £254.00 (VAT-exclusive) from a supplier

He is able to correct them on his next return.

(b) (i) Calculate the net VAT adjustment figure needed to correct these errors.

£

(ii) Identify the impact on VAT of each error.

	Impact on VAT
Invoice 1	▼
Invoice 2	▼

Picklist options:

Increase output tax
Increase input tax
Decrease output tax
Decrease input tax

Joseph wants to correct only Invoice 2.

(iii) Are the following statements true or false?

	True	False
I should follow Joseph's instructions as he is the business owner.		
I should disclose both errors to HMRC without Joseph's consent.		
I should make Joseph aware that deliberate underpayment of VAT is tax evasion which is a crime.		

Task 5 (12 marks)

This task is about verifying VAT returns.

(a) **Identify whether the following statements about where transactions are entered on a VAT return are true or false.**

	True	False
VAT on sales returns reduces VAT payable so should be included in Box 4 of the VAT return		
Overseas sales of goods are included in the total for Box 6 of the VAT return		
The VAT on purchase of services from overseas suppliers will only be included in Box 1 of the VAT return		

Florence Ltd is registered for VAT, making both standard-rated and zero-rated supplies. The company's accounting systems are separate from its Making Tax Digital-compliant tax software on which its VAT returns are prepared. Florence Ltd operates the annual accounting scheme (making monthly VAT payments) and is preparing its VAT return for the year ended 30 September 20X1 ready for submission.

The company's VAT payable in respect of the year ended 30 September 20X0 was £50,000, of which £4,000 was the balancing payment.

You work in the accounts department of Florence Ltd and the financial controller has asked you to prepare a reconciliation of the VAT return to the trial balance to confirm the accuracy of the figures prior to the submission of the return.

The draft VAT return for the period contains the following figures:

	£
Box 1	235,600.00
Box 4	(182,200.00)
Box 5	53,400.00
Box 6	1,325,000
Box 7	945,000

The VAT payable in the trial balance as at 30 September 20X1 is £7,800 and the following figures have been extracted from the nominal ledger:

	£
B/fwd	4,000.00
Paid	(49,000.00)
Output VAT	235,000
Input VAT	(182,200)
C/fwd	7,800.00

On investigation, you find that a credit note issued to a customer with a VAT inclusive value of £3,600 was omitted when entering information in the VAT return software.

(b) (i) Identify TWO reasons why the VAT liability on the draft VAT return differs from the VAT payable on the trial balance.

	✓
Output VAT on the VAT return is incorrect due to the credit note	
The accounting systems are incorrect due to the credit note	
The company has made payments on account of its VAT liability during the year	
The VAT software has not taken into account the payment on the prior year's balancing payment of VAT	

(ii) Complete the table below to reconcile the figure in the draft VAT return to the figure in the trial balance. Use a minus sign or brackets where appropriate.

	£
Amount due per draft VAT return	
▼	
▼	
VAT payable per the trial balance	7,800.00

Picklist options:

Payments on account in respect of the year ended 30 September 20X1
Output VAT on credit note issued
Balancing payment in respect of the year ended 30 September 20X0
Value of credit note issued

(iii) Identify the correct action that you should now take

	✓
Correct the VAT return and submit it	
Put a journal entry through the accounts to correct the trial and submit the VAT return as it is	
Correct the VAT return and ask the financial controller to review it	
No further action is required	

Task 6 (11 marks)

This task is about VAT rules on record keeping, filing and payment/repayment, including non-compliance implications.

Georgina is a client of your firm of accountants. She has recently started to trade running a convenience store, under the busines name "Quick Bits". All of Georgina's customers pay for their goods immediately by cash or card payment. She has registered for HMRC's online services and recently registered for VAT but she is worried about the administrative burden that registration will place on her business and potential penalties for failing in her obligations. She has asked your firm for advice regarding what she will need to do to register for Making Tax Digital, and for details of special schemes that may reduce her compliance burden.

Georgina is planning to pay her VAT by direct debit.

(a) **Identify FOUR pieces of information that Georgina will require in order to register for Making Tax Digital.**

	✓
Georgina's home address	
Georgina's National Insurance number	
The business address of Quick Bits	
Her VAT registration number	
Her Government Gateway user ID and password	
The business's e-mail address	

(b) (i) **Complete the following statement concerning Georgina's compliance obligations under the standard scheme:**

A VAT return will be required every [▼   ] and will be due within

[▼   ] of the end of the VAT period. Georgina's VAT liability will be

collected [▼   ] .

Picklists:

1. Month
   3 months
   year

2. 1 month
   1 month and 7 days
   2 months

3. On the same day as the return is due
   3 days after the return is due

(ii) **Identify TWO consequences for Georgina of filing three VAT returns late in a twelve month period. Assume the payment of the associated VAT liabilities was also late and the annual turnover of Quick Bits is £100,000.**

	✓
A Surcharge Liability Notice would be issued to Georgina	
Georgina would be liable to a penalty of 5% of the third late payment (waived if less than £400)	
Georgina would be liable to a penalty of 2% of the second late payment (waived if less than £400)	
Georgina would be liable to a penalty of 2% of the third late payment (waived if less than £400)	
Georgina would be charged a late filing penalty of £100 per late return	
Georgina would be charged interest on the underpaid VAT	

(c)   Identify the reasons that the following schemes may be suitable for Georgina:

	Impact on VAT
Flat rate scheme	▼
Annual accounting scheme	▼

Picklist:

VAT is only paid to HMRC when customers have paid
Fewer VAT returns to prepare and longer preparation period given
More straightforward calculation of VAT liability
Potentially higher VAT liability
Use of Making Tax Digital not required

Task 7 (12 marks)

(a)   Complete the following statements regarding PAYE forms:

A form [▼] is a year-end summary of pay, tax and NIC to be provided to an employee. It must be provided to the employee by [▼] following the end of the tax year.

A form [▼] is a form showing taxable benefits that have not been taxed through PAYE. It must be provided to the employee by [▼] , and a copy must be submitted to HMRC by [▼] .

Picklist:

P60
P11D
P45
31 May
6 July
6 July
P11D(b)
22 July

Mohammed won the Lottery in March 2021 and decided to employ a nanny to care for his young children and a full-time gardener. The nanny will be paid more than the earnings threshold for NIC but the gardener will not.

Each of Mohammed's two employees will be paid weekly and their first pay-day will be 7th June 2021.

(b)   **Indicate whether the following statements are true or false in respect of Mohammed's employees:**

	True	False
Mohammed cannot be required to register for PAYE as he is an individual employing people for household duties		
Mohammed will have one Full Payment Submission (FPS) to file with HMRC per month		

Arlind is employed by Trigger Plc.

The following details are shown on Arlind's payslip for the month of October:

	£
Salary	3,500
Bonus	500
Employee minimum pension contribution	750
Income tax	440
Employee national insurance contributions	384
Employer national insurance contributions	450

(c) Complete the following table in respect of Arlind's pay for October:

	£
Gross pay	
Taxable pay	
Net pay	

Task 8 (8 marks)

It is April 2022.

You work in the finance department of Fipps Ltd. Martin Goodman, your line manager, is the financial controller and can approve business payments up to £5,000 (a larger payment than this amount requires the approval of Amanda Freeman, the finance director). Donna Fipps is the business owner and makes all recruitment decisions.

All payroll taxes are paid electronically.

The company has recently recruited a new sales director, Desiree, and she will start to work for Fipps Ltd on 1 June 2022 after she has worked her notice period at her previous employment.

You have been asked to set up Desiree on the company's payroll system.

a) **Identify TWO documents that you will need to accurately input relevant information about Desiree into your payroll system.**

	✓
A tax tables book for the tax year 2022/23	
Desiree's contract of employment with Fipps Ltd	
Desiree's tax return for 2021/22	
Desiree's Form P45 from her previous employment	

HMRC have sent your department the tax codes for existing employees. One of the junior members of staff in your department has asked you to explain what they are for.

(b)   **Identify the purpose of a tax code**

	✓
To allow the employer to deduct the correct amount of income tax	
To allow the employer to deduct the correct amount of national insurance contributions	
To allow the employer to deduct the correct amount of income tax and national insurance contributions	
To inform employees about the rate of tax they will pay	

Fipps Ltd has entered into a PAYE Settlement Agreement in respect of a party held for its employees during the tax year 2021/22 and you have calculated the National Insurance due thereon as £2,675.

(c)   (i)   **Complete the following memo in respect of the PAYE Settlement Agreement**

Class [▼] (1) National Insurance of £2,675 is due in respect of the staff party. This tax must be paid by [▼] (2).

If the National Insurance is not paid on time, the company will be liable to an initial penalty of [▼] (3) after [▼] (4).

Picklist:

1.   1
       1A
       1B

2.   19 July 2022
       22 July 2022
       19 October 2022
       22 October 2022

3.   2
       5
       10
       15

4.   7 days
       30 days
       6 months
       12 months

(ii)   **Identify to whom you should forward the completed memo.**

	✓
Martin Goodman	
Amanda Freeman	
Donna Phipps	
HMRC	

BPP PRACTICE ASSESSMENT 2

Tax Processes for Businesses FA 2021

ANSWERS

Tax Processes for Businesses (TPFB)
BPP practice assessment 2

Task 1

(a)

	✓
Assisting overseas businesses in complying with UK VAT regulations	
The collection and administration of VAT from UK registered businesses	✓
The calculation of VAT liabilities for UK registered businesses	
Creation of UK VAT law	

(b)

Zero-rated supplies	Traders making this type of supply usually generate refunds of input tax
Standard-rated supplies	The rate of tax on this type of supply is 20%
Exempt supplies	Traders making only this type of supply are not permitted to register for VAT
Supplies outside the scope of VAT	These supplies have no effect on the VAT calculation

(c) (i)

£	12,500

Sales are deemed to be VAT inclusive. £75,000 × 20/120 = £12,500

(ii) John's penalty for late registration will be between **0%** and **30%** of the underpaid VAT

John made an unprompted disclosure within 12 months of the VAT being due and his late registration was not deliberate

---

Task 2

(a)

	True	False
The basic tax point for goods is when an order is received.		✓

Receipt of an order is never a tax point.

(b)

	True	False
A VAT invoice must include certain details including the supplier's VAT registration number, the total VAT payable and a description of the goods supplied.	✓	
A less detailed invoice may be issued if the VAT-inclusive proceeds are less than £150.		✓
Modified invoices are made for all sales with a value of less than £250 and must include the total VAT-inclusive selling price.		✓

BPP LEARNING MEDIA

(c)

Supply	Net £	VAT £	Gross £
Standard rated	225.50	45.10	270.60
Standard rated	260.00	52.00	312.00
Reduced rate	650.00	32.50	682.50
Zero rate	500.00	0.00	500.00

£270.60 × 1/6 = £45.10

£260.00 × 20% = £52.00

£682.50 × 1/21 = £32.50

Note the shaded boxes would be automatically completed in the assessment

Task 3

(a)

	✓
No input VAT can be recovered.	
All input VAT can always be recovered because the company makes some taxable supplies.	
All input VAT can be recovered, provided certain de minimis limits are not exceeded.	✓

(b)

Bad debt	Eligible for bad debt relief ✓	Not eligible for bad debt relief ✓	Amount of bad debt relief available £
Moraira Ltd owes £3,000 from an invoice issued on 2 January 20X0. Xavier believes that the amount will be paid in full and so it has not been written-off in the accounts.		✓	0.00
Calpe Ltd owes £2,000 from an invoice issued on 15 May 20X0. Xavier does not expect that the amount will be paid and so it has been written-off in the accounts.	✓		333.33

(c)

Expense	Recover input tax ✓	Blocked input tax ✓	Partly blocked input tax ✓	Amount of VAT recoverable £
Xavier purchased a car for his own use (see above), costing £14,000.		✓		0.00
Xavier paid fuels costs of £470 in the quarter in respect of his own car			✓	70.50 (w)
Xavier purchased a car costing £9,000 for the use of his employees, for business journeys only. The car is kept at the business' premises overnight.	✓			1,800.00

Working: £470 × 20% × 1,500/2,000

Task 4

(a)

	✓
The VAT payment for the previous period of £2,400 has not been entered in the VAT account.	✓
The VAT payment for the previous period of £2,400 has been entered twice in the VAT account.	

If the payment for the previous period had been posted in the VAT account, the liability showing would be £8,000.00 – £2,400.00 = £5,600.00 ie the liability for the current period.

If the previous payment had been entered twice, the balance showing on the VAT account would have been too low by £2,400.00 ie would have been £3,200.00.

(b) (i)

£	629.20

(£3,400 × 20%) – (£254 × 20%)

(ii)

	Impact on VAT
Invoice 1	Increase output tax
Invoice 2	Increase input tax

(iii)

	True	False
I should follow Joseph's instructions as he is the business owner.		✓
I should disclose both errors to HMRC without Joseph's consent.		✓
I should make Joseph aware that deliberate underpayment of VAT is tax evasion which is a crime.	✓	

Task 5

(a)

	True	False
VAT on sales returns reduces VAT payable so should be included in Box 4 of the VAT return		✓
Overseas sales of goods are included in the total for Box 6 of the VAT return	✓	
The VAT on purchase of services from overseas suppliers will only be included in Box 1 of the VAT return		✓

(b) (i)

	✓
Output VAT on the VAT return is incorrect due to the credit note	✓
The accounting systems are incorrect due to the credit note	
The company has made payments on account of its VAT liability during the year	✓
The VAT software has not taken into account the payment on the prior year's balancing payment of VAT	

(ii)

	£
Amount due per draft VAT return	53,400.00
Payments on account in respect of the year ended 30 September 20X1	(45,000.00)
Output VAT on credit note issued	(600.00)
VAT payable per the trial balance	7,800.00

Prior year VAT liability = £50,000. Monthly payments on account of £5,000 × 9 = £45,000.

(iii)

	✓
Correct the VAT return and submit it	
Put a journal entry through the accounts to correct the trial and submit the VAT return as it is	
Correct the VAT return and ask the financial controller to review it	✓
No further action is required	

Task 6

(a)

	✓
Georgina's home address	
Georgina's National Insurance number	✓
The business address of Quick Bits	
Her VAT registration number	✓
Her Government Gateway user ID and password	✓
The business's e-mail address	✓

(b) (i) A VAT return will be required every **3 months** and will be due within **1 month** and 7 days of the end of the VAT period. Georgina's VAT liability will be collected **3 days after the return is due.**

(ii)

	✓
A Surcharge Liability Notice would be issued to Georgina	✓
Georgina would be liable to a penalty of 5% of the third late payment (waived if less than £400)	
Georgina would be liable to a penalty of 2% of the second late payment (waived if less than £400)	
Georgina would be liable to a penalty of 2% of the third late payment (waived if less than £400)	✓
Georgina would be charged a late filing penalty of £100 per late return	
Georgina would be charged interest on the underpaid VAT	

As Quick Bit's turnover is less than £150,000, the first default within the SLN period (ie the second late payment) does not incur a penalty. The third pate payment triggers a 2% penalty but this is not charged if the penalty is less than £400.

Interest is only charged where a VAT liability is understated.

(c)

	Impact on VAT
Flat rate scheme	More straightforward calculation of VAT liability
Annual accounting scheme	Fewer VAT returns to prepare and longer preparation period given

Task 7

(a)   A form **P60** is a year-end summary of pay, tax and NIC to be provided to an employee. It must be provided to the employee by **31 May** following the end of the tax year.

A form **P11D** is a form showing taxable benefits that have not been taxed through PAYE. It must be provided to the employee by **6 July,** and a copy must be submitted to HMRC by **6 July.**

(b)

	True	False
Mohammed cannot be required to register for PAYE as he is an individual employing people for household duties		✓
Mohammed will have one Full Payment Submission (FPS) to file with HMRC per month		✓

Mohammed will have to file a FPS form every week as this is the frequency by which he pays his employees.

(c)

	£
Gross pay	4,000
Taxable pay	3,250
Net pay	2,426

Workings

- Gross pay (3,500 + 500) = £4,000

- Taxable pay (3,500 + 500 – 750) = £3,250

- Net pay (3,500 + 500 – 750 – 440 – 384) = £2,426

Task 8

(a)

	✓
A tax tables book for the tax year 2022/23	
Desiree's contract of employment with Fipps Ltd	✓
Desiree's self-assessment tax return for the tax year 2021/22	
Desiree's Form P45 from her previous employment	✓

Tax tables will not be necessary as the payroll software should be automatically updated by the software provider. Desiree's contract of employment should contain her personal details and salary information. Desiree's tax return for the previous year is not relevant to payroll deductions. Her P45 will contain details of pay in April and May 2022, which is necessary for the payroll software to calculate the correct tax deductions.

(b)

	✓
To allow the employer to deduct the correct amount of income tax	✓
To allow the employer to deduct the correct amount of national insurance contributions	
To allow the employer to deduct the correct amount of income tax and national insurance contributions	
To inform employees about the rate of tax they will pay	

(c) (i)

Class **1B** National Insurance of £2,675 is due in respect of the staff party. This tax must be paid by **22 October 2022**.

If the National Insurance is not paid on time, the company will be liable to an initial penalty of **5%** after **30 days**.

(ii)

	✓
Martin Goodman	✓
Amanda Freeman	
Donna Phipps	
HMRC	

BPP PRACTICE ASSESSMENT 3

Tax Processes for Businesses FA 2021

Time allowed: 1 hour and 30 minutes

Tax Processes for Businesses (TPFB)
BPP practice assessment 3

Task 1 (9 marks)

(a) Indicate whether the following businesses are making taxable supplies or not taxable supplies.

	Taxable supplies ✓	Not taxable supplies ✓
G plc, which sells pet insurance (an exempt supply)		
Alain, who sells children's car seats (a reduced-rated supply)		

It is 31 December.

Julian has been trading for ten months and his taxable turnover has consistently been £7,500 per month. Next month's turnover is expected to be the same.

Jasper has been trading for ten months and his taxable turnover has consistently been £6,500 per month. Today he received an order for taxable supplies of £80,000 to be invoiced on 20 January, in addition to his normal monthly turnover.

(b) (i) **Indicate whether Julian should register for VAT immediately or monitor his turnover and register later.**

	✓
Register immediately	
Monitor turnover and register later	

(ii) **Indicate the date by which Jasper should inform HMRC of his requirement to register for VAT and the date from which he will be registered for VAT by HMRC.**

Jasper must inform HMRC of his requirement to register	▼
Jasper will be registered for VAT from	▼

Picklist 1:

Immediately
By 30 January
By 31 January

Picklist 2:

31 December
20 January
1 February

Gomez Ltd uses the annual accounting scheme. The business's VAT liability for the year ended 30 June 20X0 was £150,000 and for the following year, the year ended 30 June 20X1 was £185,000.

(c) (i) The final balancing payment for the year ended 30 June 20X1 is:

	✓
£Nil	
£35,000	
£50,000	
£185,000	

(ii) The final balancing payment is due by:

	✓
30 June 20X1	
30 July 20X1	
31 July 20X1	
31 August 20X1	

The directors of Gomez Ltd expect its taxable turnover for the year ended 30 June 20X2 to be approximately £1,650,000.

(iii) Indicate what action Gomez Ltd should take in respect of its growing taxable turnover

	✓
Switch to quarterly accounting for VAT from the quarter ended 30 September 20X1	
Monitor taxable turnover for the year ended 30 June 20X2 and exit the annual accounting scheme as soon as taxable supplies exceed £1,600,000	
Monitor taxable turnover for the year ended 30 June 20X2 and exit the annual accounting scheme on 30 June 20X2 if taxable supplies exceed £1,600,000 for the year	
Apply to enter the cash accounting scheme	

Task 2 (8 marks)

(a) Identify whether the statements below are true or false.

	True	False
VAT paid by a business on their purchases and expenses is called output tax		
Sales of goods and services made by a business are called outputs		

A registered trader receives an order for goods on 15 June 20X1. The trader delivers the goods to the customer on 20 June 20X1, and issues an invoice on 23 June 20X1. The customer pays for the goods in full on 2 July 20X1.

(b) (i) Identify the tax point for this transaction.

	✓
15 June 20X1	
20 June 20X1	
23 June 20X1	
2 July 20X1	

(ii) Identify the tax point if the goods had been supplied by the trader on a sale or return basis

	✓
20 June 20X1	
23 June 20X1	
2 July 20X1	
20 June 20X2	

(c) Identify with a tick which TWO of the following do not need to be included on a valid (full) VAT invoice.

	✓
VAT number of supplier	
Invoice date	
VAT number of customer	
Rate of VAT	
Total price excluding VAT for each type of item	
Total amount of VAT for each type of item	
Total price including VAT for each type of item	
Name and address of customer	
Name and address of supplier	

(d) A trader makes a standard-rated supply with a VAT-inclusive value of £3,600.00. The trader uses the flat rate scheme and the relevant percentage for his business is 13%.

Complete the following sentences. Enter figures in pounds and pence.

(i) The VAT payable to HMRC by the trader is

£ [ ]

(ii) The trader retains net sales income of

£ [ ]

£

Task 3 (12 marks)

(a) Indicate whether the following statement is true or false.

	True	False
A business makes supplies that are both standard-rated and zero-rated. All of the input VAT can be reclaimed providing certain (*de minimis*) conditions are met.		

(b) For each of the VAT registered businesses below:

    (i) Identify whether the following input tax can be recovered, or is blocked.

    (ii) Calculate the amount of input tax which can be recovered. Round down figures to the nearest penny. If your answer is zero, enter '0.00'.

	Recover input tax ✓	Blocked input tax ✓	Input tax that can be recovered £
Juliet works as a sole trader and uses the flat rate scheme for VAT. She purchases a van for use in her business costing £5,200 inclusive of VAT at the standard rate.			
Juliet works as a sole trader and uses the flat rate scheme for VAT. She purchases goods for resale in her business costing £5,000 exclusive of VAT.			
Jamil is a partner in a partnership. The partnership does not use any special schemes. It purchases a car for use by Jamil for both business and private use, costing £7,500 plus VAT.			
Jamil is a partner in a partnership. The partnership does not use any special schemes. The partnership spends £2,675 inclusive of VAT at the standard rate on entertaining overseas clients.			

Finlay runs a VAT registered business and provides a company car and fuel to his sales manager for both business and private use. The car has CO2 emissions of 190g/km.

During the quarter ended 30 June 20X1, the sales manager drove 3,500 miles, for which Finlay incurred petrol costs of £528 inclusive of VAT. 2,100 miles were for business journeys.

(c) Indicate which TWO of the following treatments would be acceptable in Finlay's VAT return in respect of the VAT on the fuel costs.

	✓
Reclaim the full £88 input tax incurred	
Reclaim £52.80 input tax	
Reclaim £88 of input tax and enter £68.17 in output tax as a fuel scale charge	
Recover no input tax and enter £68.17 in output tax as a fuel scale charge	

Task 4 (8 marks)

(a) **Identify whether the following statement is true or false.**

	True	False
When a trader receives a credit note from a supplier VAT payable by the trader will increase.		

The VAT account at the end of a period shows the correct VAT liability of £3,000.00. The VAT return shows a liability of £3,600.00.

(b) **Which ONE of the following could explain the difference?**

	✓
Bad debt relief (VAT of £300.00) has been included as output tax rather than input tax on the return.	
A VAT refund from the previous period of £600.00 has been included as input tax on the VAT return.	

Victoria made several errors on her last VAT return. She needs to inform HMRC in writing preferably by completing form 652 'Notification of Errors in VAT Returns'.

(c) **Identify with a tick any of the following statements that could be correct in relation to the errors.**

	✓
The error is less than the error correction reporting threshold, but deliberate.	
The error is less than the error correction reporting threshold, but not deliberate.	
The error is more than the error correction reporting threshold, and deliberate.	
The error is more than the error correction reporting threshold, but not deliberate.	

A UK registered business both buys and sells standard-rated goods to and from businesses in France. It does not use postponed accounting for imports.

(d) **Which TWO of the following statements are correct?**

	✓
UK VAT will be paid on imports via the business's VAT return.	
UK VAT will be paid on imports at their point of entry into the UK.	
The UK business will charge the French standard VAT rate to the buyer.	
The UK business will not charge 20% UK VAT on its sales.	

Task 5 (12 marks)

This task is about verifying VAT returns.

Rochica runs a VAT-registered business and has recently started to prepare her own VAT returns, having previously paid an accountant to prepare them.

She has asked for your advice concerning how certain transactions should be reflected on her VAT return.

(a)   Identify whether the following VAT figures should appear in Box 1 and/or Box 4 of Rochica's VAT return

	Box 1 ✓	Box 4 ✓
VAT incurred on the purchase of fixed assets		
VAT on credit notes received from suppliers		
VAT on the purchase of services from an overseas supplier		
VAT charged on reduced-rate supplies to customers		

Rochica has discovered some errors relating to the information she had provided to her accountant in relation to her previous VAT return. The errors relate to the omission of a cash sale for £5,000 of standard-rated goods and £14,000 of reduced rated goods from her accounting system. She also failed to record a purchase invoice for goods of £2,000 in her accounting system. All figures are exclusive of VAT at the standard rate.

(b)   (i)   Complete the following information in respect of each invoice, showing its impact on Rochica's previously declared VAT liabilities.

	Impact on VAT
Cash sale omission	▼
Purchase Invoice omission	▼

Picklist:

output tax understated
input tax understated
output tax overstated
input tax overstated

(ii)   Calculate the net error from the previous VAT return. Enter your answer to the nearest penny.

£ _____

(iii)   Assuming Rochica's error can be corrected by adjusting her current VAT return, show the effect of correction of the error.

	Adjustment
Box 1	▼
Box 4	▼

Picklist:

Increase
Decrease
no effect

(c) Identify TWO implications of Rochica deciding not to correct her VAT return for the net error.

	✓
A penalty of up to 70% of the underpaid VAT	
Interest will be charged on the underpaid VAT	
Rochica's accountant will be liable to HMRC for the underpayment	
A penalty of up to 30% of the underpaid VAT	

Task 6 (11 marks)

This task is about VAT rules on record keeping, filing and payment/repayment, including noncompliance implications.

(a) Identify whether the following statements about VAT legal requirements are true or false

	True	False
The surcharge system for late payment of VAT is more lenient for businesses with turnover over £150,000		
Penalties for errors may be reduced by HMRC if the taxpayer makes an unprompted disclosure		
A surcharge liability notice will be removed if the taxpayer files their next VAT return and pays their VAT on time		
Where a business fails to register for VAT, HMRC will raise an assessment estimating the business's VAT liability and this estimate becomes the final VAT liability.		

Terrance is VAT registered and files quarterly VAT returns. He does not use any special schemes. His annual turnover is £250,000.

Having previously submitted all his VAT returns and paid his tax on time, Terrance has recently struggled with the administrative side of his business. His four most recent VAT returns have been submitted as follows:

Quarter ended	VAT liability £	Return filing and VAT payment date
31 March 20X1	12,000	15 May 20X1
30 June 20X1	15,000	31 August 20X1
30 September 20X1	11,000	28 October 20X1
31 December 20X1	19,000	17 February 20X2

(b) For each of the VAT returns outlined above, calculate the amount of penalty Terrance will incur. If there is no penalty, enter 0.00

	Penalty £
31 March 20X1	
30 June 20X1	
30 September 20X1	
31 December 20X1	

Terrance is concerned that some of his VAT records may have been accidentally destroyed when he cleared out his home office.

(c) Indicate which THREE of the following records are required to be kept by Terrance for VAT purposes.

	✓
Terrance's personal bank account statements	
Terrance's business bank account statements	
Details of goods imported from overseas by Terrance for his personal use	
Invoice for the purchase of a machine 8 years ago, used in Terrance's business on which Terrance reclaimed input VAT	
Invoices issued to customers relating to exempt supplies made by Terrance	
Records relating to the export of goods by Terrance to overseas customers	

Task 7 (12 marks)

This task is about the principles of payroll.

(a) Indicate whether the following statements about payroll administration are true or false

	True	False
Payslips only need to show the number of hours worked if pay varies depending on time worked		
A PAYE settlement agreement is where an employer comes to an agreement with HMRC to pay over their PAYE bill late		
The taxable value of non-cash benefits (e.g. company car) is shown on the P60 end of year certificate		
Small employers with average monthly PAYE payments of less than £1,500 can chose to pay annually		
Payroll records for 2021/22 must be kept until 5 April 2025.		

Jammy Bakery Ltd has 7 employees who each have use of a company van. Jammy Bakery pays its class 1A National Insurance liability in respect of this benefit electronically.

(b) (i) The deadline for payment of the Class 1A NIC liability is [▼]

(ii) This year, the payment was made 2 months late. The penalty suffered for this late

payment is [▼] of the Class 1A NIC due

Picklist 1:

22 July
22 April
22 October

Picklist 2:

1%
5%
10%

(c) **Which FIVE of the following are the main functions of payroll software?**

	✓
Calculating PAYE and NIC liabilities	
Calculating statutory pay	
Completing employee tax returns	
Recording employee details	
Complying with GDPR	
Salary reviews	
Reporting payroll information to HMRC	
Calculating pay and deductions	

Task 8 (8 marks)

This task is about communicating information on VAT.

Reply to Holly Field's email giving her the information she has requested

To:	Accounts assistant
From:	Holly Field
Subject:	Impact of a rise in the VAT rate
Date:	17 July 20X1

I have been listening to the news recently and have heard there may be a rise in the standard rate of VAT from 20% to 25%.

I am extremely concerned as to how this will affect my business. Most of my sales are direct to the general public, so I am unsure whether to increase my prices to take account of the proposed new rate, or to try and keep them the same.

Would you mind explaining the consequences of these two options for me?

Your speedy response would be much appreciated,

Holly

(a) **You are required to reply to Holly, filling in the missing details of the email below.**

EMAIL

To: Holly Field
From: Accounts assistant
Subject: Impact of a rise in the VAT rate
Date: 20 July 20X1

Dear Holly,

Thank you for your email requesting details of how the proposed rise in the standard rate of VAT might affect your business.

As you quite rightly say, you could [＿＿＿＿＿▼] (1), which means effectively, you as a business will suffer the impact of the increased rate. Alternatively, you could

[＿＿＿＿＿▼] (1) resulting in your customers having to pay extra, which in itself, may lead to the loss of revenue.

For example with the present rate of VAT at 20% if you want to make income of £100 on a

sale you will charge your customers £ [＿＿＿▼] (2).

With a proposed rise to 25% you can either:

- [＿＿＿＿＿▼] (3) to your customer, which will still leave you £100; or

- [＿＿＿＿＿▼] (3) for your customers, leaving you only £96 after output VAT is charged (£120 × 100/125).

This is a decision that you will need to give careful thought to, but I hope this clarifies the situation for you.

Kind regards

Accounts Assistant

Picklist:

(1)
could keep your prices the same
increase your prices

(2)
100
120

(3)
charge £125 (£100 plus 25% VAT)
keep your price at £120

(b) **Identify two sources of information that will enable you to verify the correct VAT rate applicable to Holly's supplies.**

	✓
VAT legislation on the gov.uk website	
Holly's customers	
Holly's tax software provider	
Advice from HMRC's VAT helpline	

BPP PRACTICE ASSESSMENT 3

Tax Processes for Businesses FA 2021

ANSWERS

Tax Processes for Businesses (TPFB)
BPP practice assessment 3

Task 1

(a)

	Taxable supplies ✓	Not taxable supplies ✓
G plc, which sells pet insurance (an exempt supply)		✓
Alain, who sells children's car seats (a reduced-rated supply)	✓	

(b)   (i)

	✓
Register immediately	
Monitor turnover and register later	✓

Taxable supplies to date are £75,000, which is under the compulsory registration threshold

(ii)

Jasper must inform HMRC of his requirement to register	immediately
Jasper will be registered for VAT from	31 December

As taxable supplies will be approximately £86,500 in the next 30 days, Julian is required to register under the future test. He will be registered from the start of the 30-day period and so must charge VAT on his taxable supplies straight away.

(c)   (i)

	✓
£Nil	
£35,000	
£50,000	✓
£185,000	

£185,000 − (£150,000 × 90%)

(ii)

	✓
30 June 20X1	
30 July 20X1	
31 July 20X1	
31 August 20X1	✓

(iii)

	✓
Switch to quarterly accounting for VAT from the quarter ended 30 September 20X1	
Monitor taxable turnover for the year ended 30 June 20X2 and exit the annual accounting scheme as soon as taxable supplies exceed £1,600,000	
Monitor taxable turnover for the year ended 30 June 20X2 and exit the annual accounting scheme on 30 June 20X2 if taxable supplies exceed £1,600,000 for the year	✓
Apply to enter the cash accounting scheme	

Task 2

(a)

	True	False
VAT paid by a business on their purchases and expenses is called output tax		✓
Sales of goods and services made by a business are called outputs	✓	

(b) (i)

	✓
15 June 20X1	
20 June 20X1	
23 June 20X1	✓
2 July 20X1	

The basic tax point (delivery date) of 20 June is replaced by the actual tax point (invoice date) of 23 June as the invoice is issued within 14 days of the basic tax point.

(ii)

	✓
20 June 20X1	
23 June 20X1	
2 July 20X1	✓
20 June 20X2	

Goods on sale or return have a tax point of the earlier of their adoption (2 July 20X1, as the payment in full of the invoice is an indicator that the customer has adopted the goods) or 12 months after their delivery (20 June 20X2)

(c)

	✓
VAT number of supplier	
Invoice date	
VAT number of customer	✓
Rate of VAT	
Total price excluding VAT for each type of item	
Total amount of VAT for each type of item	
Total price including VAT for each type of item	✓
Name and address of customer	
Name and address of supplier	

(d) (i)   The VAT payable to HMRC by the trader is £468.00

13% × £3,600.00

(ii)   The trader retains net sales income of £3,132.00

£3,600 – £468

Task 3

(a)

	True	False
A business makes supplies that are both standard-rated and zero-rated. All of the input VAT can be reclaimed providing certain (*de minimis*) conditions are met.		✓

The *de minimis* test is applied when a trader makes taxable and **exempt** supplies.

(b)

	Recover input tax ✓	Blocked input tax ✓	Input tax that can be recovered £
Juliet works as a sole trader and uses the flat rate scheme for VAT. She purchases a van for use in her business costing £5,200 inclusive of VAT at the standard rate.	✓		866.66
Juliet works as a sole trader and uses the flat rate scheme for VAT. She purchases goods for resale in her business costing £5,000 exclusive of VAT.		✓	0.00

BPP LEARNING MEDIA

	Recover input tax ✓	Blocked input tax ✓	Input tax that can be recovered £
Jamil is a partner in a partnership. The partnership does not use any special schemes. It purchases a car for use by Jamil for both business and private use, costing £7,500 plus VAT.		✓	0.00
Jamil is a partner in a partnership. The partnership does not use any special schemes. The partnership spends £2,675 inclusive of VAT at the standard rate on entertaining overseas clients.	✓		445.83

Because Juliet uses the flat rate scheme, the only input VAT she can recover is on the purchase of fixed assets costing over £2,000.

(c)

	✓
Reclaim the full £88 input tax incurred	
Reclaim £52.80 input tax	✓
Reclaim £88 of input tax and enter £68.17 in output tax as a fuel scale charge	✓
Recover no input tax and enter £68.17 in output tax as a fuel scale charge	

As detailed mileage records were kept by the sales manager, Finley can choose to either:

(1) recover input tax on the business miles only (£528 × 20/120 × 2,100/3,500) = £52.80 or alternatively

(2) use the fuel scale charge system; this requires him to charge £409 × 20/120 = £68.17 in output tax on his VAT return but the full input tax incurred of £88 will be recoverable.

Task 4

(a)

	True	False
When a trader receives a credit note from a supplier VAT payable by the trader will increase.	✓	

(b)

	✓
Bad debt relief (VAT of £300.00) has been included as output tax rather than input tax on the return.	✓
A VAT refund from the previous period of £600.00 has been included as input tax on the VAT return.	

(c)

	✓
The error is less than the error correction reporting threshold, but deliberate.	✓
The error is less than the error correction reporting threshold, but not deliberate.	
The error is more than the error correction reporting threshold, and deliberate.	✓
The error is more than the error correction reporting threshold, but not deliberate.	✓

(d)

	✓
UK VAT will be paid on imports via the business's VAT return.	
UK VAT will be paid on imports at their point of entry into the UK.	✓
The UK business will charge the French standard VAT rate to the buyer.	
The UK business will not charge 20% UK VAT on its sales.	✓

Task 5

(a)

	Box 1 ✓	Box 4 ✓
VAT incurred on the purchase of fixed assets		✓
VAT on credit notes received from suppliers		✓
VAT on the purchase of services from an overseas supplier	✓	✓
VAT charged on reduced-rate supplies to customers	✓	

(b)   (i)

	Impact on VAT
Cash sale omission	output tax understated
Purchase invoice omission	input tax understated

(ii)   **£1,300.00**

£5,000 × 20% + £14,000 × 5% – £2,000 × 20%

(iii)

	Adjustment
Box 1	Increase
Box 4	no effect

A single adjustment is made for the net of all the errors – in this case output VAT will be increased by the net error of £1,300.

(c)

	✓
A penalty of up to 70% of the underpaid VAT	✓
Interest will be charged on the underpaid VAT	✓
Rochica's accountant will be liable to HMRC for the underpayment	
A penalty of up to 30% of the underpaid VAT	

Task 6

(a)

	True	False
The surcharge system for late payment of VAT is more lenient for businesses with turnover over £150,000		✓
Penalties for errors may be reduced by HMRC if the taxpayer makes an unprompted disclosure	✓	
A surcharge liability notice will be removed if the taxpayer files their next VAT return and pays their VAT on time		✓
Where a business fails to register for VAT, HMRC will raise an assessment estimating the business's VAT liability and this estimate becomes the final VAT liability.	✓	

(b)

	Penalty £
31 March 20X1	0.00
30 June 20X1	0.00
30 September 20X1	0.00
31 December 20X1	950.00

No penalty arises in respect of the quarter ended 31 March 20X1 - as this is Terrance's first late filing he is issued with a Surcharge Liability Notice (SLN). The penalty for the quarter ended 30 June 20X1 is 2% of the VAT paid late (£300), but is not charged as it is less than £400. The return for the quarter ended 30 September 20X1 was filed on time. The second default (ie the late return and payment for the quarter to 31 December 20X1) results in a penalty of 5% of the VAT liability of £19,000, £950.00, and is charged as it is more than £400.

(c)

	✓
Terrance's personal bank account statements	
Terrance's business bank account statements	✓
Details of goods imported from overseas by Terrance for his personal use	
Invoice for the purchase of a machine 8 years ago, used in Terrance's business on which Terrance reclaimed input VAT	
Invoices issued to customers relating to exempt supplies made by Terrance	✓
Records relating to the export of goods by Terrance to overseas customers	✓

Task 7

(a)

	True	False
Payslips only need to show the number of hours worked if pay varies depending on time worked	✓	
A PAYE settlement agreement is where an employer comes to an agreement with HMRC to pay over their PAYE bill late *A PAYE settlement agreement is where an employer agrees to pay an employee's income tax on certain benefits*		✓
The taxable value of non-cash benefits (e.g. company car) is shown on the P60 end of year certificate *The taxable value of non-cash benefits is shown on the P11D*		✓
Small employers with average monthly PAYE payments of less than £1,500 can chose to pay annually *Small employers with average monthly PAYE payments of less than £1,500 can chose to pay quarterly*		✓
Payroll records for 2021/22 must be kept until 5 April 2025.	✓	

(b) (i)   The deadline for payment of the Class 1A NIC liability is **22 July**

(ii)   This year, the payment was made 2 months late. The penalty suffered for this late payment is **5%** of the Class 1A NIC due

(c)

	✓
Calculating PAYE and NIC liabilities	✓
Calculating statutory pay	✓
Completing employee tax returns	
Recording employee details	✓
Complying with GDPR	
Salary reviews	
Reporting payroll information to HMRC	✓
Calculating pay and deductions	✓

ANSWERS

Task 8

(a)

EMAIL

To: Holly Field
From: Accounts assistant
Subject: Impact of a rise in the VAT rate
Date: 20 July 20X1

Dear Holly,

Thank you for your email requesting details of how the proposed rise in the standard rate of VAT might affect your business.

As you quite rightly say, you │ **could keep your prices the same** │, which means effectively, you as a business will suffer the impact of the increased rate. Alternatively, you could │ **increase your prices** │, resulting in your customers having to pay extra, which in itself, may lead to the loss of revenue.

For example, with the present rate of VAT at 20% if you want to make income of £100 on a sale you will charge your customers £ │ **120** │.

With a proposed rise to 25% you can either:

- │ **charge £125 (£100 plus 25% VAT)** │ to your customer, which will still leave you £100; or

- │ **keep your price at £120** │ for your customers, leaving you only £96 after output VAT is charged (£120 × 100/125).

This is a decision that you will need to give careful thought to, but I hope this clarifies the situation for you.

Kind regards

Accounts Assistant

(b)

	✓
VAT legislation on the gov.uk website	✓
Holly's customers	
Holly's tax software provider	
Advice from HMRC's VAT helpline	✓

Tax Processes for Business (Level 3) reference material

Finance Act 2021 – for assessments from September 2022 to December 2023

Reference material for AAT assessment of Tax Processes for Businesses

Introduction

This document comprises data that you may need to consult during your Tax Processes for Businesses computer-based assessment.

The material can be consulted during the sample and live assessments through pop-up windows. It is made available here so you can familiarise yourself with the content before the test.

Do not take a print of this document into the exam room with you*.

This document may be changed to reflect periodical updates in the computer-based assessment, so please check you have the most recent version while studying. This version is based on Finance Act 2021 and is for use in AAT Q2022 assessments in 2022 and 2023.

*Unless you need a printed version as part of reasonable adjustments for particular needs, in which case you must discuss this with your tutor at least six weeks before the assessment date.

Contents

1 Rates of VAT

Taxable supplies:

Standard rate	20%
Reduced rate	5%
Zero rate	0%

Non-taxable supplies have no VAT applied:

- Exempt
- Outside the scope of VAT

2 Registration and deregistration for VAT

Registration threshold	£85,000
Deregistration threshold	£83,000

- A business **can** register for VAT if it is making taxable supplies.
- If at the end of any month taxable turnover for the previous 12 months is more than the current registration threshold, the business **must** register for VAT within 30 days.

  Registration without delay is required if, at any time, the value of taxable turnover in the next 30-day period alone is expected to be more than the registration threshold.
- If taxable turnover for the previous 12 months is less than the deregistration threshold, or if it is expected to fall below it in the next 12 months, a business can deregister.
- A registration must be cancelled within 30 days if the business ceases to make taxable supplies.

3 Failure to register for VAT

- This can result in a penalty for failure to notify. The penalty is a % of potential lost revenue (PLR):

Type of behaviour	Within 12 months of tax being due		12 months or more after tax was due	
	unprompted	prompted	unprompted	prompted
Non-deliberate	0–30%	10–30%	10–30%	20–30%
Deliberate	20–70%	35–70%	20–70%	35–70%
Deliberate and concealed	30–100%	50–100%	30–100%	50–100%

- Penalties will not be applied if there is a reasonable excuse.
- HMRC will treat the business as though it had registered on time and will expect VAT to be accounted for as if it had been charged. The business has two choices:
  - i. treat the invoices as VAT inclusive and absorb the VAT which should have been charged, or
  - ii. account for VAT as an addition to the charges already invoiced and attempt to recover this VAT from its customers.

BPP
LEARNING
MEDIA

4 Changes to the VAT registration

HMRC must be notified of a change of:

Name, trading name or address	Within 30 days
Partnership members	Within 30 days
Agent's details	Within 30 days
Bank account details	14 days in advance
Change in business activity	Within 30 days

5 Keeping business and VAT records

Record retention period	6 years
Penalty for failure to keep records	£500

6 Contents of a VAT invoice

The required content of VAT invoice depends on whether it is:

- A full invoice
- A simplified invoice – supplies of less than £250
- A modified invoice – retail supplies of more than £250

Invoice information	Full invoice	Simplified invoice	Modified invoice
Unique invoice number that follows on from the last invoice	Yes	Yes	Yes
Supplier's name and address	Yes	Yes	Yes
Supplier's VAT number	Yes	Yes	Yes
Date	Yes	No	Yes
The tax point (if this is different from the invoice date)	Yes	Yes	Yes
Customer's name or trading name, and address	Yes	No	Yes
Description of the goods or services	Yes	Yes	Yes
Total amount excluding VAT	Yes	No	Yes
Total amount of VAT	Yes	No	Yes
Price per item, excluding VAT	Yes	No	Yes
Quantity of each type of item	Yes	No	Yes
Rate of any discount per item	Yes	No	Yes
Rate of VAT charged per item – if an item is exempt or zero-rated make clear no VAT on these items	Yes	Yes	Yes
Total amount including VAT	No	Yes	Yes

7 Partial exemption for VAT

De minimis amount	£625 per month
Proportion of total input VAT	<50%

- Generally, partially exempt business cannot reclaim the input tax paid on purchases that relate to exempt supplies.
- If the amount of input tax incurred relating to exempt supplies is below a minimum de minimis amount, input tax can be reclaimed in full.
- If the amount of input tax incurred relating to exempt supplies is above the de minimis amount, only the part of the input tax that related to non-exempt supplies can be reclaimed.

8 International trade and VAT

Export of goods	Zero-rated
Import of goods	UK VAT applied at: • Port of entry; or • Postponed accounting
Export of services	Apply UK VAT if place of supply is in the UK: • For supplies to business, place of supply is the location of the customer (no UK VAT) • For supplies to non-business customers, place of supply is the location of the supplier (charge UK VAT).
Import of services	Reverse charge applies

9 Tax points for VAT

Basic tax point date	Date of despatch of the goods/carrying out of the service
Actual tax point date may be earlier	If either: • Payment is received earlier • Invoice is issued earlier Actual tax point becomes the earlier of these two dates.
Actual tax point date may be later	If: • Invoice is issued within 14 days of despatch/ service (and advance payment didn't apply)

- Deposits are treated separately to final payment and so may have a different tax point.

- The tax point is always the date of payment if cash basis is being applied.

- Where services are being supplied on a continuous basis over a period in excess of a month but invoices are being issued regularly throughout the period, a tax point is created every time an invoice is issued or a payment is made, whichever happens first.

- Goods on sale or return will have a tax point date either on adoption (the customer indicates they will keep the goods) or 12 months after removal of the goods where this is earlier.

10 Time limits for issuing a VAT invoice

- Within 30 days of tax point which is either:
  - within 30 days of date of supply or
  - within 30 days of payment if payment was in advance.

11 Blocked expenses and VAT

Input VAT cannot be recovered on blocked expenses.

Business entertainment

- The exception is that input tax can be reclaimed in respect of entertaining overseas customers, but not UK or Isle of Man customers.

- When the entertainment is in respect of a mixed group of both employees and non-employees (e.g. customers and/or suppliers), the business can only reclaim VAT on the proportion of the expenses that is for employees and on the proportion for overseas customers.

Cars

- Input VAT can only be recovered on cars if it is wholly for business (no private use).

- 50% of input VAT can be recovered when cars are hired/leased.

- VAT can be recovered on commercial vehicles such as vans/lorries.

Assets with private use

- The VAT recovery should be based only on the proportion related to business use.

12 Fuel scale charge and VAT

If the business pays for road fuel, it can deal with the VAT charged on the fuel in one of four ways:

- reclaim all of the VAT. All of the fuel must be used only for business purposes.

- reclaim all of the VAT and pay the appropriate fuel scale charge (see below) – this is a way of accounting for output tax on fuel that the business buys but that is then used for private motoring

- reclaim only the VAT that relates to fuel used for business mileage. Detailed records of business and private mileage must be kept

- do not reclaim any VAT. This can be a useful option if mileage is low and also if fuel is used for both business and private motoring. If the business chooses this option it must apply it to all vehicles, including commercial vehicles.

- The fuel scale charge is as follows:

Description of vehicle: vehicle's CO_2 emissions figure	VAT inclusive consideration for a 12 month prescribed accounting period (£)	VAT inclusive consideration for a 3 month prescribed accounting period (£)	VAT inclusive consideration for a 1 month prescribed accounting period (£)
120 or less	585	145	48
125	875	219	72
130	936	233	77
135	992	247	82
140	1,053	262	87
145	1,109	277	91
150	1,170	292	97
155	1,226	306	102
160	1,287	321	106
165	1,343	336	111
170	1,404	350	116
175	1,460	364	121
180	1,521	379	126
185	1,577	394	130
190	1,638	409	136
195	1,694	423	141
200	1,755	438	145
205	1,811	453	150
210	1,872	467	155
215	1,928	481	160
220	1,989	496	165
225 or more	2,045	511	169

- Where the CO_2 emission figure is not a multiple of 5, the figure is rounded down to the next multiple of 5 to determine the level of the charge.

BPP
LEARNING
MEDIA

13   Bad debts and VAT

VAT that has been paid to HMRC and which has not been received from the customer can be reclaimed as bad debt relief. The conditions are that:

i.   the debt is more than six months and less than four years and six months old

ii.   the debt has been written off in the VAT account and transferred to a separate bad debt account

iii.   the debt has not been sold or handed to a factoring company

iv.   the business did not charge more than the normal selling price for the items.

Bad debt relief does not apply when the cash accounting scheme is used because the VAT is not paid to HMRC until after the customer has paid it to the supplier.

14   Due dates for submitting the VAT return and paying electronically

Deadline for submitting return and paying VAT – quarterly accounting	1 months and 7 days after the end of the VAT period
Deadline if being paid by direct debit	HMRC will collect 3 working days after the submission deadline.

- Please see alternative submission and payment deadlines for special accounting schemes.

15   Special accounting schemes for VAT

15.1   Annual accounting scheme for VAT

Joining the scheme	Maximum (estimated) taxable turnover in next 12 months	£1.35m
Leaving the scheme	Compulsory if taxable turnover at the end of the VAT accounting year exceeds the threshold	£1.6m
VAT returns	One annual return	2 months after the end of the accounting period
VAT payments (monthly)	Nine monthly interim payments (10% of estimated VAT bill based on previous returns)	At the end of months 4 to 12 in the accounting period.
	Balancing payment	2 months after the end of the accounting period
VAT payments (quarterly)	Three interim payments (25% of estimated VAT bill based on previous returns)	At the end of months 4, 7 and 10 in the accounting period
	Balancing payment	2 months after the end of the accounting period

15.2 Cash accounting scheme for VAT

Joining the scheme	Maximum (estimated) taxable turnover in next 12 months	£1.35m
Leaving the scheme	Compulsory if taxable turnover at the end of the VAT accounting year exceeds the threshold	£1.6m

15.3 Flat Rate Scheme for VAT

Joining the scheme	Taxable turnover (excluding VAT) in the next 12 months	£150,000
Leaving the scheme	On the anniversary of joining, turnover in the last 12 months (including VAT) or expected turnover in next 12 months	£230,000
Discount	In first year of being VAT-registered	1%
Limited cost business	Goods cost less than either: • 2% of turnover, or • £1,000 a year	16.5%
Capital expenditure	Input tax can be recovered on individual large capital purchases	£2,000

- The appropriate flat rate % will be provided in the assessment.

16   Errors in previous VAT Returns

- Adjustments can be made to correct errors that are:
    - below the reporting threshold
    - not deliberate
    - for an accounting period that ended less than 4 years ago.

- The reporting threshold is:
    - £10,000 or less or
    - up to 1% (maximum £50,000) of total value of sales and all other outputs excluding any VAT
- When the next VAT return is submitted, the net value is added to VAT due on sales and other outputs for tax due to HMRC, or to VAT reclaimed in the period on purchases and other inputs for tax due to you.
- If the value of the net VAT error discovered is above the reporting threshold, it must be declared to HMRC separately, in writing.

17 Late filing and late payment of VAT

A default is recorded if:

- A VAT return is not filed by the deadline.
- Full payment is not paid by the deadline.

On the first default, a 12-month 'surcharge period' commences. If another default is made during this time:

- the surcharge period is extended for a further 12 months
- a surcharge may apply
- The surcharge is a percentage of the VAT outstanding on the due date for the accounting period that is in default.

Defaults within surcharge period	Surcharge if annual turnover is less than £150,000	Surcharge if annual turnover is £150,000 or more
1st	No surcharge	2% (no surcharge if this is less than £400)
2nd	2% (no surcharge if this is less than £400)	5% (no surcharge if this is less than £400)
3rd	5% (no surcharge if this is less than £400)	10% or £30 (whichever is more)
4th	10% or £30 (whichever is more)	15% or £30 (whichever is more)
5th or more	15% or £30 (whichever is more)	15% or £30 (whichever is more)

18 Assessments of VAT

If a VAT Return is not submitted on time, HMRC will issue a 'VAT notice of assessment of tax' which will state how much HMRC think is owed.

If HMRC issue an assessment that is too low, a 30% penalty can be charged for not telling them it is incorrect within 30 days.

There is a £400 if a paper VAT return is submitted, unless HMRC has given an exemption from online submission.

19 Penalties for inaccuracies in VAT return

A penalty can be charged as a percentage of the potential lost revenue (PLR):

Type of behaviour	Unprompted disclosure %	Prompted disclosure %
Careless	0–30	15–30
Deliberate	20–70	35–70
Deliberate and concealed	30–100	50–100

20 Interest charged on VAT

Interest may be charged if:

- Less VAT is reported than is actually due
- An assessment is paid which is lower than the actual VAT due
- An error was made on a previous return resulting in an underpayment of VAT.

Interest is charged at 2.6%.

21 Payroll record retention

Retention period	3 years
Penalty for failure to maintain records	£3,000

22 Types of payroll submission

Full Payment submission (FPS)

- File on or before employees pay day.
- Include payments to and deductions for all employees.

Employer payment summary (EPS)

- File if no employees were paid in the month.
- Send by the 19th of the following tax month.

23 Payroll deadlines

Registering for PAYE	You must register before the first payday. You cannot register more than 2 months before you start paying people.
Month end date for PAYE	5th of each month
Payment date for monthly payroll	22nd of each month if paid electronically. 19th otherwise. If monthly amounts are <£1,500, quarterly payments can be made.

Provide employees with P60	31st May
Filing deadline for Expenses & Benefits forms	6th July
PAYE and Class 1A NIC payment date	22nd July if paying electronically. 19th July otherwise.
PAYE settlement agreement submission date	31st July
PAYE and Class !B NIC payment date	22nd October if paying electronically. 19 October otherwise.

24 Penalties for late submission of payroll filings

Penalties may apply if:

- the FPS was late
- the expected amount of FPS's was not filed
- an EPS was not filed

Number of employees	Monthly penalty
1 to 9	£100
10 to 49	£200
50 to 249	£300
250 or more	£400

Penalties may not apply if:

- The FPS is late but all reported payments on the FPS are within three days of the employees' payday (unless there is regular lateness).
- A new employer is late but sends the first FPS within 30 days of paying an employee.
- It is a business's first failure in the tax year to send a report on time.

25 Penalties for late payroll payment

Late payment of monthly/quarterly payments

- The first failure to pay in a tax year does not count as a default.
- Late payment penalties apply to late payments and payments of less than is due.

Number of defaults in a tax year	Penalty percentage applied to the amount that is late in the relevant tax month
1 to 3	1%
4 to 6	2%
7 to 9	3%
10 or more	4%

Additional penalties will apply if:

| A monthly or quarterly amount remains outstanding after 6 months | 5% of unpaid tax |
| A monthly or quarterly amount remains outstanding after 12 months | A further 5% of unpaid tax |

These additional penalties apply even where only one payment in the tax year is late.

Late payments of amounts due annually or occasionally

30 days late	5%
6 months late	Additional 5%
12 months late	Additional 5%

26 Penalties for inaccuracies in payroll filings

A penalty can be charged as a percentage of the potential lost revenue (PLR):

Type of behaviour	Unprompted disclosure. %	Prompted disclosure. %
Careless	0–30	15–30
Deliberate	20–70	35–70
Deliberate and concealed	30–100	50–100